COWORKING INC.

THE BOHEMIAN MOVEMENT THAT ADOPTED CAPITALISM

Jonathan O'Byrne

Editor: Karen Rowe

Cover Design: Daliborka

Inside Layout: Ljiljana Pavkov

ISBN: 978-1-64370-714-3 (international trade paper edition)

ISBN: 978-1-64370-715-0 (ebook)

Dedicated to people brave enough to leave comfort behind in search of a brighter future.

TABLE OF CONTENTS

COWORKING INC.
THE BOHEMIAN MOVEMENT
THAT ADOPTED CAPITALISM

ACKNOWLEDGEMENTS

It takes a team to publish a book and I would like to start by thanking my publishing team: Thank you Karen Rowe for getting me over the line, Rebecca Pillsbury for the heavy lifting. I would also like to thank Andrew Griffiths for inspiring me to write in the first place.

The journey of the past few years that led to the writing of this book wouldn't have been possible without the love and support of my biological and work families. To my parents and brother, thank you for your unending support. To my incredible coworking team that bring light to my daily life and help me deliver my vision, thank you.

Esther, Lina, Aslinda, Nadia, Nancy, Sean, Jessica, Nelly, Waheeda, Seha, Maria, Larissa, Ivy & Hitan

To my dear friends and support system: Oran, Danielle, Sal, Adele, Tim, Joanne, Elle.

And to my research assistants whose hard work helped me substantiate my theories with hard data: Alain, Molly & Elegance.

INTRODUCTION

WHY *COWORKING INC.*?

Coworking is unquestionably the most exciting sociological development in real estate in the last several hundred years. I know 'exciting real estate' could sound like a contradiction in terms, but to those interested in property and human psychology, coworking is a genuine object of fascination. Only once in a few generations does a disruptor of this magnitude come along.

Coworking has disrupted every aspect of our relationships with our built environment. It has challenged our values around ownership, tenancy, public and private space. But for something that is so important, it is so poorly understood. I wrote *Coworking Inc.* to fill the informational void around coworking and to orientate those interested to the movement.

In 2010, what had been a small grassroots movement hit a tipping point. Coworking grew and transformed into a professional industry with tremendous momentum and impact. This transformation wasn't an accident; it was the result of a perfect storm of events that I will explore in this book and use as an avenue to help readers understand the driving macro trends behind the industry.

The title of this book alludes to the commercialization of a highly social movement. In a few short years, coworking went from being a minor blip in the real estate industry to a force that represents a significant percentage of the office space in the world's most important cities. In 2017, JLL (Jones Lang LaSalle, an investment management company) reported that 8 percent of all newly built office real estate in London had been occupied by coworking operators.

For such an important and transformational movement, surprisingly little has been published. Furthermore, what has been published was written by observers on the periphery of the industry and has rapidly gone out of date. So far, almost nothing has been written by people on the cutting edge of the movement: coworking operators.

I am one of those people. In 2012, I founded Singapore's first coworking space in the downtown commercial core known colloquially as the CBD (Central Business District). I chose the core because, even then, I could see how coworking could cater to businesses beyond the startup community. In the ensuing six years, I rapidly grew my coworking environments and in 2016 I joint ventured with one of the largest real estate companies in Asia.

I wrote this book for the disrupted. I wrote this book for landlords, property owners and corporate real estate professionals who manage large portfolios and large groups of people to help them understand how their landscape is being reshaped, in real time, right in front of them.

My hope is that by fostering better understanding between asset owners, large portfolio managers and operators we may be able to truly unlock the potential of the world's sleeping real estate assets. My theories and analysis of coworking, the basis of what *Coworking Inc.* puts forward for consideration, were born out of my first-hand experience of the industry, the thousands of hours and millions of dollars I have invested designing, building and operating coworking businesses, as well as out of my own private research and investigation.

As you will come to discover, I have a deep curiousity with the human experience. Coworking to me represents a right-sizing of our physical environment with our ideological one - an opinion I hope you will come to share with me by the end of this book.

THIRTY-TWO YEARS AWAY FROM HOME

Immediately after graduating from university, I moved from London to Oman in a deliberate attempt to get out of the line of fire of the financial crisis. I landed a great job in Oman managing communications for a multi-billion-dollar corporate. The role provided wonderful exposure and I really enjoyed my job.

However, in 2010, only a year after I began my new job, my partner at the time was offered a dream job in Singapore. We agreed between the two of us that we'd both move to Singapore. It had been easy for me to get a job in Oman and integrate into a community there, so I figured the transition to living and working in Singapore would be no different. I had no understanding of just how hard it would be.

At twenty-four years old, I was much younger than most of the other expatriates in Singapore and I had landed without a job or a community with an established moral and social code. Because of my employment history of relative seniority and strong income so soon after graduating, finding a new position proved very challenging. In a culture where age is perceived to very closely correlate with a person's worth, I was an outlier: a very expensive twenty-something from a far-away land. Outliers are quite difficult to employ; they don't generally fit into boxes.

Unwilling to accept the status quo, I started my own agency - a communications studio - from my guest bedroom. I retained my previous employer in Oman as my first client. I picked up a local film producer, an interior decorator and a couple of other clients and developed a successful small business. The company grew into a six-figure business within two years. At the same time,

I found myself in possibly the darkest place emotionally that I've ever been.

In stark contrast to my move to Oman, my move to Singapore was defined not only by the loss of my community in Oman but by the complete absence of a new community upon my arrival. In Oman, I'd worked for a company that had 2,000 employees. When employees move with a corporate employer and join a big organisation, they become part of a corporate family. That opportunity really eases the move, because until those employees form their own social relationships, they have business relationships to help feed part of their soul.

When I moved to Singapore, I worked alone. Moving overseas to start one's own business as opposed to moving within a company is such a stark difference in terms of being able to adjust to a new community. Even though I'd moved for the person I loved, I was by myself most of the time because my partner, who worked in finance, was putting in sixteen- to eighteen-hour work days. I woke up alone. I had breakfast alone, lunch alone and dinner alone. My partner came home, slept and went back to work.

It didn't take long to realise I was not the only one in that position. I would attend bank events with my partner and meet amazing trailing partners who were very intelligent people. I remember meeting the ex-head of HR at Barclays followed by an ex-banker at J.P. Morgan. I said to the latter, 'What do you do?' He said, 'I play golf.' Then the ex-head of HR at Barclays said, 'I drive my kids to school.' It killed me. These were people with MBAs and master's degrees and they were basically sitting on their hands because the environment they'd entered into was so unstable they couldn't find employment.

The challenge with being self-employed is that it's incredibly difficult to build community. I had no children (the great social enablers), so therefore no reason to interface with a large swath of the expatriate community. I wasn't single, so there was little reason to go to bars or clubs. If you don't have a family, then you truly are an island of one.

With a few years' hindsight and a few psychometric profiles under my belt, I can tell you I'm quite an extrovert. I now know I need to have people around me, but at the time I was stubborn enough to think I could go it alone - and to be honest, I didn't have many other options. I worked alone those two years; on one occasion while on a deadline for a client, I didn't leave the house for four consecutive days. My closest interaction was with my personal trainer, who I didn't even like all that much.

It was a very special kind of torture to be that isolated. After two years in Singapore, I knew almost nobody. I was significantly depressed, my beautiful apartment felt like an ivory prison and I realised no amount of income was going to fix what I was going through. What made matters worse was there was nothing I could do, nowhere I could go, no network I could join that would replace the community I had lost. Literally, I was either going to leave my partner, leave Singapore, or do something worse. I realised I was in a really bad place and I had to change it.

I had become so dissatisfied with working from home that I decided to find an alternative. I thought that a business centre sounded ideal – there would be a lot of other companies and connections to make and people to meet. There are dozens of business centres in Singapore, so I just needed to find the one that felt right.

How wrong I was. I spent months and looked at over thirty business centres of varying quality, style and location. It didn't matter where I looked; I kept finding the same beige rooms with long corridors that led nowhere. I never once saw clients speaking to each other. Often, meeting rooms were empty and unused. It was like visiting a pet shop with each puppy contained in an illuminated habitat, isolated from the other puppies next door and possibly even totally unaware of their existence.

With each viewing, I became more and more angry. Singapore is expensive; I was shown offices that were US$3,000 or $4,000 a month for one person. They were beautiful spaces, but they were basically beige boxes with frosted glass. I didn't speak to a single other person besides the salesperson as I went through each space. I didn't see anybody. The community spaces were little pantry areas which had nobody in them. I thought, 'I'll pay all of this money to be here and I still won't meet anybody.'

I grew increasingly frustrated. Then a turning point occurred. As I left another of these hateful storage containers one morning, I happened to catch sight of the name board just outside the lobby. I paused to read the list of companies in the space. That particular centre contained a hedge fund, several lawyers, a life coach, a well-known Silicon Valley tech company, a notorious female venture capitalist who had just been featured in the Business Times, independent stock traders, oil companies, engineering firms, marketing agencies and more.

I was dumbfounded. These were exactly the people I wanted to meet! This name board was a Rolodex of potential clients, partnerships and collaborations. But in this centre, those connections would never happen. I can so vividly recall the deep sense of injustice, wastefulness and sheer frustration that boiled within me. I couldn't get over how nobody could see the incredible things that could be achieved if these people just *spoke* to each other.

It blew my mind that no one had created a space for collaboration. Brilliant people were locking themselves away in expensively appointed private offices and isolating themselves from the entire value of a shared office: the fact that it is shared.

THE SOLUTION TO TWO PROBLEMS

One of the challenges I faced when I had a home-based business was I lived in an environment of false economics. I had almost no costs, so a disproportionate amount of my revenue was profit. When I considered a serviced office, I would suddenly be taking on massive overheads. So large, in fact, that I would have had to grow my business by three or four people just to offset the increased operating costs of an office.

There had to be a way to give somebody a logical progression, I thought. The client could opt-in, opt-out, work part-time and scale incrementally. What used to be a fixed operating cost needed to be turned into a variable expense. What if we turned physical space into a subscription - Real Estate as a Service? The idea consumed me to the point that I shut down my agency after two years, recycling the profits and assets of that business and using them to build my first coworking environment.

I designed my coworking environment from a needs perspective. Then, I tried to build a business case to make it financially viable. I had a strong idea of what a business would be happy to pay per head. I intimately understood the client because I was the client.

I bet everything on it. I opened the business with a five-figure monthly rent and no clients because I was so adamant it needed to exist. From the day the business opened its doors in December, I knew that it had until May before I would be in deep financial trouble. I had a five-month runway to get the business off the ground, before I lost everything. As it turned out, not only did I get it off the ground, but by June it was full and by September two more floors were added.

The new business became Collective Works, which for a time was Singapore's largest and fastest growing coworking environment. We made a name for ourselves catering to high-performing business leaders. In the four years since its launch, Collective Works grew from 2,500 to over 30,000 square feet and it now comprises a community of over 200 companies. Through my business I have supported members from forty-seven countries and helped over 1,400 people make Singapore their business and personal home.

My decision to start the business the way I did may sound risky, but from my perspective it felt like I was making a measured bet. I knew a collaborative coworking environment needed to exist. Coworking is an entirely different beast to serviced offices and business centres. Unlike serviced offices and business centres, where each business is closed away in an independent office, coworking environments are often open and designed to encourage collaboration and community building in what is termed 'accelerated serendipity.'

In my experience in public relations, I learned that a practitioner's value is determined by who they know, or the size of their network. Who one knows provides a pretty accurate measure of how socially adept he or she is, how credible that person is as an opinion former and the scope of their influence. After all, if someone is going to be paid to talk a good game for their clients, that service is only worth paying for if they have some expensive ears listening.

The more time I spend with business leaders, the more I believe that the old adage, 'it's who you know not what you know,' is incredibly important in business. The most successful business people I know are collectors: they collect brilliant people, nurture those relationships and inspire them to work with them. I have also noticed that brilliant people usually know each other and they can sniff out an imposter better than most of us can sniff out bad milk.

Before anyone can recognize the value of a business, before partnerships can be forged, before networks can be shared and before knowledge can be leveraged, business leaders first have to be able to connect with relevant communities. If they aren't in an environment that promotes networking and interaction, then those connections will never happen.

Since starting Collective Works in 2012, I have come to establish the theory that coworking is more than a new business model, it is a new business methodology which is disrupting the real estate industry. *Coworking Inc.* looks at the future of coworking as a method and an industry and at the broader impact it is having on the commercial infrastructure of some of the world's most important cities. It explains the origins of coworking, the factors that are driving its rapid expansion and offers some educated predictions for the future of the industry. If you don't want to miss out on what many high-profile corporate and commercial real estate leaders are catching onto, read on.

WHAT YOU THINK YOU KNOW ABOUT COWORKING IS MOST LIKELY WRONG

Despite the growing popularity of coworking, there is still much confusion about what coworking actually is. Why is there so much confusion? Coworking is still a relatively young and dynamic industry. It continues to evolve very quickly in response to the marketplace and this ongoing iteration means it can take some time for new versions to be defined and for those definitions to stick. What this means to people outside the coworking industry is that the information they are following can quickly become out of date.

The basis of the problem is that those outside the industry keep attempting to define coworking by its physicality. While that practice seems logical, attempting to define coworking by offices, desks and infrastructure fails to explain the nuance and complexity of the movement. It fails to recognize how elements of coworking have been incorporated into newly iterated business concepts with restaurants and members clubs and have even been applied to custom software.

What contributes to making coworking difficult to define is that coworking is actually a methodology. It is a way of solving complex problems with a community-based approach. It is an ecosystem-derived solution. When coworking is understood to be an intangible approach, then its rapid evolution and bespoke application suddenly begins to make sense. Coworking is being consistently applied as a logic; the outcomes are tailored to the individual situation.

Despite the incredible success companies have found by shifting to a coworking model, some asset managers love to hate coworking; they focus on the element of lease arbitrage: the fact that many coworking environments make a profit by densifying the revenue from a location to more than the square foot leasing price. However, to reduce coworking to such a simplistic form is to fail to understand the subtleties of coworking that justify those higher prices and to ignore what an incredibly positive force that space can be for the broader community. Instead of resisting change, asset managers need to shift their mindsets and get on board with this highly successful, growing phenomenon.

CLASSIFICATION OF COWORKING SPACES

First, let's clarify what I mean by coworking. Every coworking environment I have seen falls into one of these four categories: hobby space, social space, pro space or mega space.

A hobby space isn't the owner's primary business or source of income; in most cases these spaces are small, ranging from leftover desks in larger offices to smaller units.

Social spaces are networking spaces, where the primary objective is to enable discourse and idea sharing. These spaces adopt a philosophy of network first, work second. However, as someone who grew up having to finish my homework before I could go outside and ride my bike, I have always found coworking environments that prioritise social and event space over workspace to have things a bit backward. While socializing is incredibly important, socializing without business or without a structure, context, purpose, or reason is just hanging out - and I know very few successful people who spend their days regularly hanging out.

Pro spaces, the third category of coworking environments, are the ones that focus on work. These are primary workspaces, environments designed to empower business leaders. They are designed from the start to function as work spaces that adopt a philosophy of work first, socialize second. Pro spaces are usually run by a dedicated team whose focus is to make the space as high-performing as possible.

Mega spaces are a new evolution of the pro space. They are huge installations, typically 40,000 square feet or larger and can house hundreds of members. These spaces can incorporate both pro space and social space elements in a single installation because their scale allows them to do so. They are designed as primary workspaces and professionally operated by teams of people. Most recently, additional ecosystem elements have started to be included in these spaces such as restaurants, bars, gyms and other facilities.

The types of coworking environments I will focus on throughout this book are pro spaces and mega spaces. I feel these have the best capability to address the current challenges of both small and big business and to pave the way to the coworking industry of the future.

THE COWORKING METHODOLOGY

In February 2016 at Coworking Unconference Asia, I delivered a keynote address to a gathered audience of Asian coworking professionals entitled 'Coworking 2.0: The Coworking Pivot.' It was a keynote designed to address the rapid pace of change in the industry and the palpable difference since the industry hit its pivot point and became a significant global trend. The presentation was also intended to confront coworking operators' mindsets around coworking being purely a real estate product.

The main message of my address was that coworking is not a business, nor is it a real estate product. Coworking is an approach to solve problems. That was the first time I shared my theory on the coworking methodology with the industry at large and the presentation drew whoops of applause from the audience.

THE COWORKING HOLY GRAIL

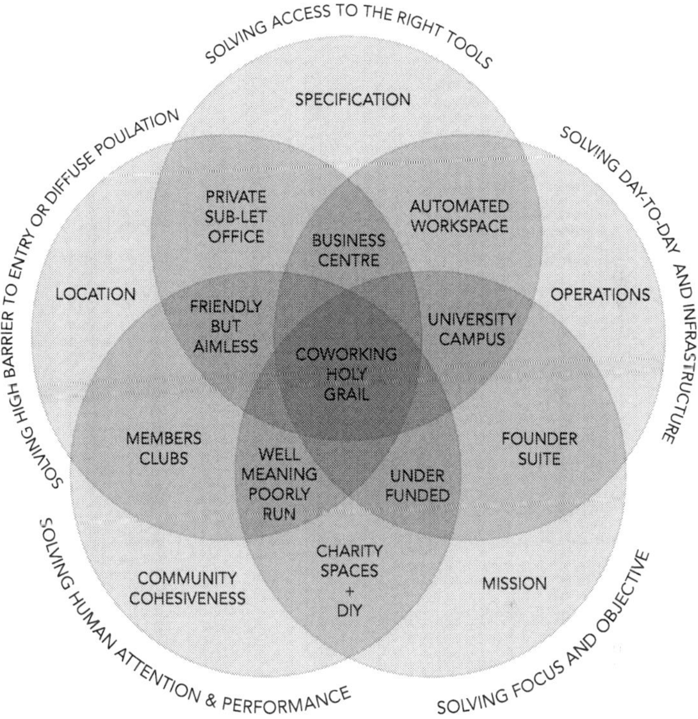

The diagram above shows the perfect execution of the coworking method as it pertains to coworking spaces. Coworking spaces require the perfect ratio of Specification, Operations, Location, Community Cohesiveness and Mission as is Necessary to solve the specific community need.

For a given market the most acute need could lie in any one of the circles in the Venn diagram. For example, in major cities one of the primary problems coworking solves is making incredibly expensive corporate real estate accessible and flexible – it gets businesses into the right *Location*. In the case of non-profits and industry specific spaces the problem coworking spaces solve is one of maintaining focus, enthusiasm and preventing mission drift - *Mission and Community Cohesiveness*. Some more socially active spaces solve the need for human connection and provide the support structure so often absent in smaller companies - *Appropriate Specification*.

Coworking is so often thought of as a physical product, a working environment where people share space and where multiple business operators co-locate for lean gains and operational efficiencies. But coworking is not actually about the physical space. Using a community-based approach, coworking has enabled buildings and companies to behave differently and that has very much disrupted the original status quo of real estate.

By pigeonholing coworking as an individual product instead of a business approach, it fails to explain why there are now so many different categories of coworking: coworking, co-living, members clubs, incubators, accelerators; all of these businesses fall under the umbrella of coworking as a broader category because they share a common methodology. With the understanding that coworking is not an outcome, we can move forward and start to look at ways that coworking can be applied to other industries and areas. And we can address some of the common misconceptions about the coworking industry.

TASK-BASED WORKING IN DRAG

One of the first misnomers of coworking is one that's being promoted by several real estate industry specialists. CBRE and JLL (two of the world's largest commercial real estate brokerages) have both published reports on the growth of coworking and its potential use within corporate environments, or what can be called internal coworking. Such a suggestion, however, indicates a misunderstanding of what coworking actually is.

Coworking is a meeting of the minds, a shared working environment between several businesses. A coworking environment just for one company is not coworking. It's mono-working.

If we go back about twelve years, there was a trend in corporate office planning that was called task-based working, which is a fancy name for hot-desking. What it meant was that based on the kind of task a person was doing, they were to use the appropriate workspace. If people were collaborating, they would stand up and be in a zone which didn't have chairs. If they were meeting with someone, they would go into a meeting room and not hold the discussion at their desk. The concept was about making offices agile and acknowledging the inefficiencies that a 1:1 ratio of desks to people creates. It was the first step toward a modern working environment.

Task-based working developed an awful reputation in corporates because it was used by many companies as a way of densifying offices. Companies suddenly realised they could take less square footage and fit more people in, so they started taking away people's desks, giving them lockers and making all of the desks hot. People didn't have regular workstations. For some people that was incredibly disruptive. Company leaders didn't realise that certain people really require a fixed workspace because all of their productivity systems are based around having the same physical space.

Task-based working was a very uncomfortable experience and because of that it has fallen out of fashion. The challenge now is that when coworking is suggested to corporate by the likes of JLL and CBRE, they are essentially re-branding task-based working and attempting to resell it. However, the primary objective with coworking is not densification; it is not reducing the square footage in one's own office. The primary objective of coworking is about fostering collaboration and the transfer of knowledge between different entities, which is why private coworking within a company doesn't work.

COWORKING IS NOT JUST FOR STARTUPS

Another big misnomer in coworking is that it is only for startups. That's just not true. A lot of this misconception comes out of the fact that coworking has been publicized and made famous by startups. Uber, for example, started in a now very famous tech incubator in Silicon Valley called Rocket Space in 2011. However, even large financial institutions such as HSBC have moved hundreds of employees into a WeWork coworking environment.

While coworking can be a great launchpad for startups, its usefulness isn't limited just to startups because startups are fundamentally businesses - they have the same requirements as mature businesses. When creating a coworking environment, it's therefore important not to create them all specifically for startup culture.

The startup culture may be one demographic of coworking, but when coworking is viewed as an approach, then it is as diverse as humanity itself. There are great coworking environments for people in almost every industry. There is a misconception that most coworking environments are for tech. In fact, media is one of the biggest sectors. At Collective Works, we have media and content creations, magazines and public relations companies and a number of creative industries. There are also some NGOs and charities and just a little bit of tech.

Another misnomer of coworking is the idea that a coworking environment is a compromise. One of the founding philosophies at Collective Works was that we wanted to create a space that was better than people could create by themselves. Using the economy of scale, we could offer greater specification, greater fit and a better working environment than companies could create themselves. Coworking, in many cases, can be a superior option to working alone and can even be a superior option to a corporate office for companies which are a lot larger.

COWORKING IS NOT CHEAP SPACE WITH A YOUTH FOCUS

Due to the trendy image of coworking, people assume that coworking environments are just for young people. Collective Works' higher-end location has a median age of thirty-two. Our original location has a median age of thirty. While that is still a young demographic, our members span a range from eighteen to fifty-seven years old, so we actually have quite a broad range of members that we look after. They are all successful business men and women who enjoy the space in different ways.

While I would say younger people are naturally gravitating to coworking by default, people who are social regardless of age will succeed. Coworking is much more about temperament and culture than it is about age. Introverts and extroverts both do well, because we're all intrinsically social people who just enjoy socializing in different amounts and in different ways.

Coworking is not a youth-focused product. One of the great examples of that is looking at the evolution of membership spaces or work clubs. There's a great coworking environment in Sydney, Australia called Work Club. The space is very focused; it has only a handful of members, but it is designed for the C-suites of some of Australia's largest companies. These are not young people but they are very successful people. Its positioning is to create a private office for them to have meetings out of their corporate offices and network at a level commiserate with their seniority - not very 'startup.'

CHAPTER ONE TAKEAWAYS

▶ Coworking is a method to solve complex problems using a community-based approach.

▶ A Coworking Space is a shared working environment used by several businesses.

▶ I see four classes of Coworking Space - Hobby, Social, Pro and Mega-Spaces; each have their own place in the market.

▶ To do coworking well you need a perfect combination of location, specification, operations, mission and community.

▶ There are great coworking environments for people in almost every industry at every price point.

▶ The goal of coworking is to create a space that is better than one business could create by itself.

▶ Coworking adoption is much more about temperament than it is about age.

▶ If there is just one company occupying the space - It might be flexible working but it isn't coworking.

ECONOMIC MODEL OF COWORKING

This chapter addresses the concerns that I hear when I introduce the concept of coworking to an audience unfamiliar with the industry. Those concerns are: Is coworking really a sustainable business model? How does it work? How is it possible to provide so much flexibility and have such high fixed-costs and still run a sustainable business?

All of these questions come down to a lack of familiarity with how coworking businesses make their money, how they curate their revenue and how they pay very careful attention to the composition of income (looking at both ad hoc, short-term income as well as fixed, recurring income). All businesses require some semblance of recurring income and coworking is no different.

In this chapter, we're going to address the concepts behind coworking, the economic environment in which coworking spaces operate and the different operating models various coworking spaces use.

CONCEPTUAL

Let's start by focusing on the concept of how a coworking space makes money. Most coworking spaces operate in a form of what's called lease arbitrage; they make the property yield more than the cost of the rent and the fixed operating costs. Good coworking operators are able to generate income in a factor of two to three times the rent on a fixed amount of space by increasing the value proposition to prospective members.

This raises the question of why companies are willing to pay two to three times more per square foot than renting space alone. Herein lies the key understanding of the coworking industry: Real estate is often one of the largest fixed costs in an organisation (after human costs), yet it is one of the lowest value adds. Tenants generally don't have a relationship with their landlords. There's very little contribution made by the building owner to improve or support the businesses that are operating within their spaces even though they represent such a massive outgoing to a company.

REAL ESTATE IS OFTEN ONE OF THE LARGEST FIXED COSTS IN AN ORGANISATION YET IT CAN ALSO BE ONE OF THE LOWEST VALUE ADDS.

A typical lease structure revolves around a bare unit being rented, renovated by the occupant and then having its renovation removed at the end of the lease term. Usually, correspondence only happens between a landlord and a tenant when there's a problem with the rental space or if a rent payment has been missed. Coworking, by contrast, is an incredibly high-touch industry. Coworking operators typically not only know the nature of their clients companies, they also know their key personnel and often each individual employee of those companies collocated in the coworking space.

In addition, coworking operators have an understanding of the demographics of their spaces: the gender ratio, the average age and a sense of what these people are interested in. Then what they do is construct a business model around those demographics, solving needs that are common within that community. I refer to this as a portfolio of revenue. At the core of a coworking product there is a membership or license fee, which is the baseline fee that's paid to an operator to use the space. But on top of that, coworking operators also focus on consolidating a share of spend.

Businesses tend to spend in a number of similar areas: They'll spend on accounting. They'll spend on employee engagement. They'll spend on hospitality. They'll spend on IT. All of these areas are functions and revenue lines for coworking spaces. However, coworking spaces also provide supporting services such as business services, virtual addressing and events and other incomes such as catering.

These added revenues wouldn't stack together without the space. The space is the base and everything else is cream on top. When these revenues are stacked, we get quite an interesting composition of spend as well as an interesting composition of income. For example, event spend would be very ad hoc and irregular and hard to forecast, but something like spend towards accounting services or virtual addressing would be fixed annual subscriptions.

One of the very first questions I'm often asked about coworking spaces is how do they make money when their clients are rolling month to month? In other words, how is risk balanced in an on-demand culture? The answer is everybody is not rolling month to month (assuming the opposite is one of the biggest misnomers in coworking). Most coworking spaces operate on a sliding scale. Price and certainty are the two key metrics. The more certainty a coworking operator is given by a client, the better the price point the client will achieve.

Typically, the most expensive way to work in a coworking space is by hot-desking or rolling up the contracts. Therefore, a significant number of clients across the space will be on six month-, twelve month-, or maybe even twenty-four- or thirty-six-month contracts, which are very similar terms to leases. Part of the skill of running a successful coworking space is getting the balance of risk and return right. If all of an operator's margin is on short-term clients, then that operator needs to make sure they have enough long-term, locked-in income that they're recovering all of their fixed overheads and therefore can afford to offer that flexibility.

When operators stack long-term recurring and short-term ad hoc income, what they get is a diversified income stream, which offers a higher margin. If they do their job right and deliver a credible product across many categories, they then expand their share of spend with their clients. As their clients begin to trust them more, the clients will also start to spend more with the operator in different areas.

What underpins this method is a concept that I call relational business. Businesses do business with people; so often this is forgotten within large organisations that do businesses with brands. Banks will use a big-four accounting firm, but in small- to medium-sized companies, that's not the case. If a client doesn't like the person in the accounting firm, the brand behind the firm doesn't matter. A coworking space is run on a concept of relational business, which is trust that is developed over time by continued performance and continued delivery.

Critically, if an operator is going to construct a business based on a portfolio of income, a share of spend and then also a risk-balance approach, what needs to be consistent across all of those areas is delivery. Clients are only going to increase their spend with an operator if they have been rewarded in every area and trust the operator fundamentally.

The final question I get on coworking incomes, on a conceptual basis, is how are coworking spaces different from business centres? What business centres do is fundamentally micro-leases of space. They focus on fractionalising a property and generating the maximum yield per square foot without building a relationship with the client. They have a physical space where they stack generic utilities such as phone lines, wifi and connectivity charges with consumables like printing charges and then perhaps front-desk secretarial services will be stacked with refreshment charges. But none of these services require a relationship or a rapport. They could be delivered in an entirely automated fashion.

When looking at a business centre's income string, generally they report yield using a per square foot metric. In coworking spaces, operators look at spend per person, which is quite a different metric because coworking spaces are focused on the individual, bearing in mind that they have in some cases a partially or significantly transient membership base who are not in the space at all times. Coworking spaces understand that a per square foot income stream is not a useful metric.

MYTH OF FLEXIBILITY

The coworking model allows a significant degree of flexibility beyond what would normally exist in a rental agreement. The myth is that such flexibility is a risk.

THE FINANCIAL ARGUMENTS OF COWORKING

1. COWORKING SPACES INCENTIVISE LOYALTY.

The longer you subscribe the better rates you get and it may surprise you that many coworking spaces have a bias towards longer term client tenures.

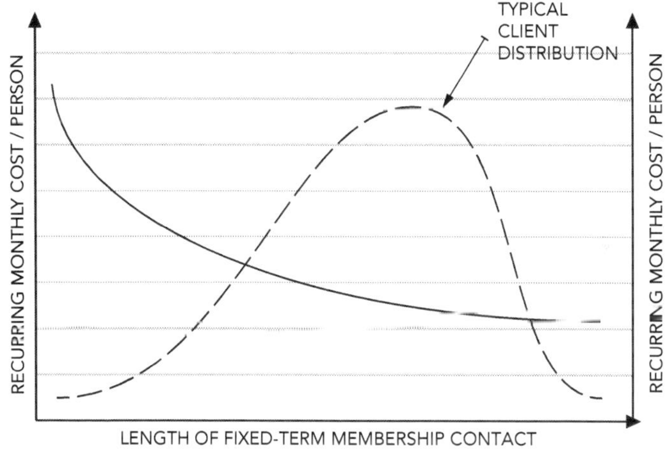

2. COMPARISON OF THE OVERHEADS OF A SCALING BUSINESS WHEN THEY LEASE VERSUS WHEN THEY LICENSE THROUGH COWORKING.

Leasing forces companies into inflexible physical space arrangements and forces a pattern of oversubscription to allow for growth. Coworking offers a linear progression.

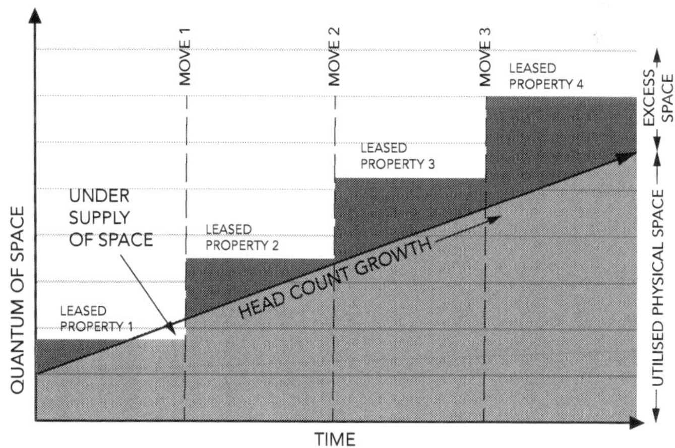

Because coworking matches 1 to 1 with employees you avoid the over subscription of space, periods of under supply as well as the inconvenience, cost and lost productivity.

The flexibility myth coincides with the old style idea that you have to lock people into contracts to get them to continue to pay you money. That model is a very old-fashioned way of doing business where operators chase long-term retainers and recurring income and then lock the relationship up contractually instead of on a performance basis.

Coworking is an incredible industry because the whole industry is performance-based. Clients subscribe to a space on flexible terms. They can vote with their feet if they're not happy with the operator's performance and what that does is hold coworking operators accountable. This model is used by the on-demand or the gig economy and was made popular by software providers. The irony is that in many ways, the flexibility in coworking actually increases retention as opposed to decreasing it.

If operators are held accountable, they are held to continued performance. Clients choose to stay with an operator because the operator has continued to perform, not because they're contractually obligated to do so. What that has led to is that, in many markets, the retention of clients in coworking spaces actually exceeds that of business centre spaces.

At Collective Works, we retain our clients for an average of twenty-seven months in a market where the industry average is only eighteen months and that's even while using flexible contract structures. A relationship that is based on mutual accountability is one that fosters trust. And apparently also great yield.

THE ECONOMIC ENVIRONMENT A SPACE OPERATES WITHIN

Coworking spaces operate within a layered economic environment. Coworking is very much a location-based product, so the first layer of coworking on a macroeconomic level is the immediate geography.

If you open a centre in a specific location, let's say a central business district (CBD) in a city, that space will automatically be compared to the other spaces that are within a kilometre radius of that space. When people choose where and how they work, geographic location is a very important component that is a function of transport links, prestige and reputation and of course lifestyle amenities and facilities that are proximate to that building.

Once the question of immediate geography has been dealt with, the next economic environment that a space needs to operate within is that of industry segmentation. Segmentation contributes to the value proposition of the space. If a space has a tightly matched segmentation with the prospective client, then it can supersede the importance of location but if it doesn't, location comes first.

To visualize this segmented landscape, have a look at the coworking segmentation matrix on the next page: where the bottom horizontal bar represents the startup level, followed by bars representing early-stage businesses, mid-stage, growth stage, medium-size companies and corporates. The vertical bars represent any industry that you can think of - finance, the arts, media and so on.

THE COWORKING SEGMENTATION MATRIX

In each market it is possible to map each operator on a matrix of stage of business and focal area. Industry agnostic operators show up horizontally, more focused ones vertically.

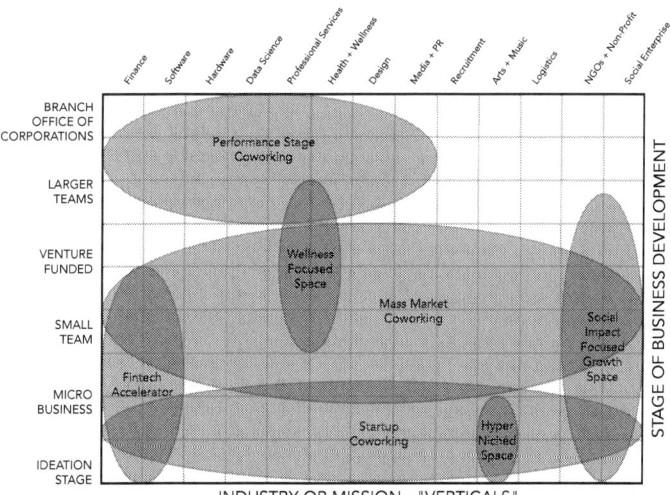

TYPICAL MATURE URBAN COWORKING MARKET DISTRIBUTION

In cities where the coworking market is starting to occupy measureable percentages of commerical real estate we can already see clear segmentation among the operators.

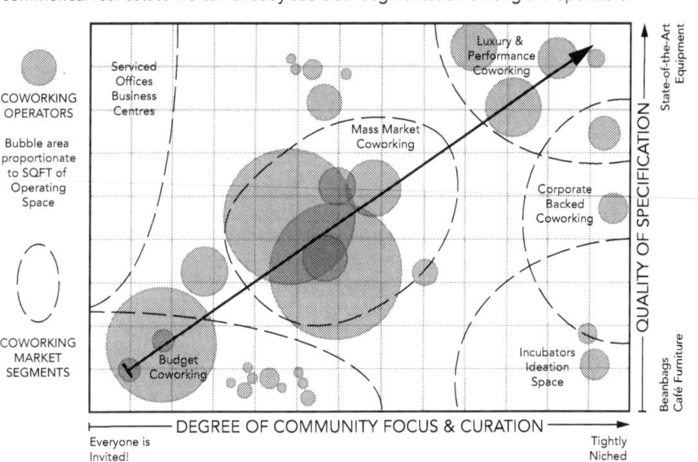

44

Now you'll see I have plotted coworking spaces onto that matrix. Some spaces are very niche, for clients at a specific horizontal stage of business or a specific vertical industry. Some spaces will focus only on horizontals, or stage of business. The most famous of these are incubators or accelerators that focus exclusively on startups. In more advanced markets like New York, London and Singapore, there are coworking spaces that focus on later-stage companies that have more advanced needs.

Coworking spaces are consolidators of businesses large and small, so they are affected by the same forces that affect their clients' businesses. When we look at the macroeconomics of a coworking space, we first have to look at the global economy. Is it open? Is it closed? Where are we in the economic, business and real estate cycle? What is happening with the local economy and how is it affected by the global economy?

For example, in global cities like London, New York, Shanghai, Singapore and Hong Kong, fluctuations in the global economy impact those markets. Fluctuations create population movement and movement in spend, so people will become more conservative or less conservative. In real estate, people often talk about a run to luxury, or a run to value, but what is talked about less is the run to flexibility. In the aftermath of the global financial crisis in 2008, what was seen in coworking was a run to flexibility; people hedging their position by avoiding long-term commitments like long leases.

THE MACROECONOMIC MODEL OF COWORKING

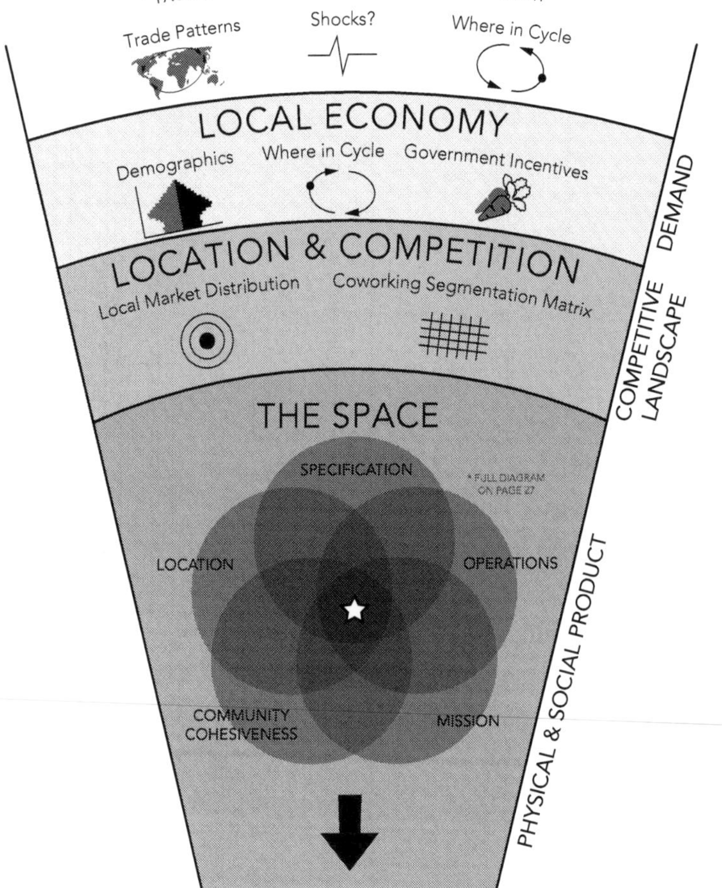

With an understanding of what's happening in the global economy, we can then look at the local economy. Look at the demographics: What are the average ages? What is the gender ratio? What is the industry make-up of that city? For example, if you are an operator trying to open a fashion or luxury goods-oriented space, Paris would be an appropriate location because it's a city with a density of talent in that field. Then you'd also want to look at local government incentives around doing business and job creation. These incentives also affect the performance of a coworking space.

The final economic environment that a coworking space operates within is its own space. This environment is the more complicated part of the economic model of coworking because for a coworking space to succeed, it needs to be successful in multiple areas. The most obvious area is in terms of design. The space needs to look and feel fantastic, but more important are composition of space (ratios of space,) and the amount of space designated to cellular office space, flexible working, collaboration, engagement and social spaces.

These spaces need to be driven by the understanding of the location, the competitive market and the local economy. For example, coworking spaces in Australia need to have much larger provisions of space per user than coworking spaces in Asia because of the local economic environment. The local economic environment in Australia lends clients to be acclimatized to having greater amounts of space. In dense Asian cities, clients are willing to accept much tighter planning and much smaller provisions of social space.

A coworking space's design informs its economic model and how it derives its revenue and that design must empathise with the local economic market. Under design, operators look at ratios of space and sophistication of fit. Major cities require a higher standard of fit than suburban ones. Operators need to look at the percentages of flexibility and agility in the design, as well as the ability of the design to be adapted on an ongoing basis. A coworking space needs to be able to respond to global and local variables in order to be successful over the long-term.

The next economic area a coworking space needs to get right in order to succeed is curation and community. Community is a word frequently thrown around by coworking spaces, but what community actually means is 'like-people'. In a high-performance community like a high-performance company, employees are put through a proven process to determine if they are like the other employees and if they're going to fit in. That is called building a corporate culture. In coworking, the question is will the client's business literally fit into the space? Do the dynamic and social forces within that company align with the social behaviours of the space?

Coworking spaces, given the close proximity of work stations and the proportions of space that are shared, need to run a similar recruitment process. They need to make sure that the clients they bring into the space are functioning similarly to the other clients in that space. Curation and community, from an economic perspective, means getting clients at the right size and stage of business, the right type in terms of temperament and from the right industry. It's important to make sure that the space has a good composition of industries, but more importantly, that the operator manages competitive forces between their clients. If they bring a competitor into a space, that's a very good way to lose a client in a flexible business model.

The final component of the economic environment is operations. Operations looks at some of the elements talked about earlier in this chapter, such as segmentation of revenue. The percentages of clients that are short-term, medium-term and long-term also align with curation because if an operator doesn't have a baseline level of clients, there is no critical mass to form a community. But from the operations side, you've got to look at the lean efficiencies: how efficiently a space operates, the number of headcounts it uses and then a performance metric on service delivery. How much value is being delivered by the operator, by the team that runs the space and by the systems that run the space?

Under operations, the key elements operators look at are efficiency and value delivery. How are they delivering the maximum amount of value, with the least amount of overhead? They need to make the most of the centre they've designed and make the most of the community they've created. When all of those elements run together, an operator has a healthy ecosystem at a centre level that sits within the physical environment of the city, the competitive environment of a city, the local economy of that part of the country and then the global economy behind it.

OPERATING MODELS

The final component to understanding the economic models of coworking is to look at the capital and corporate structuring of the spaces; in layman's terms, that is who pays for the fit-out and how the income is derived and distributed from the space.

Operating Model A: The most common model in the coworking industry right now, particularly with smaller spaces, is an owner-operated model. In an owner-operated model, a founder or a group of founders create a space. They will source the money for the capital expenditure (the funds used by a company to set up a physical business) either from themselves, from friends and family, or, if they're more sophisticated, from investors.

The relationship between the space and the building can be that the space is either leased or the operator may also own the building. There are cases where building owners start an owner-operated model to try and gentrify the yield from a building, but more commonly coworking space is leased from a building and then operated with a lease-arbitrage model beyond that. In an owner-operated model, the owner puts forward 100% of the capital expenditure; he or she will keep 100% of the profit and also bear 100% of the risk.

Operating Model B: The second operating model is known as a management contract. A management contract is the opposite of an owner-operated model. A management contract is where an operator is brought in to manage a space and provide the intellectual property and the experience and the operating manuals and standards, but provides typically little to no money towards capital expenditure.

In this model, a building owner, asset owner, or perhaps even a corporate with excess space, provides the capital for the fit-out and the renovation work and then appoints an operator as a manager on an ongoing basis who initially advises on fit-out (the operating model and colour or flavour of the space) and then pays the manager an ongoing service fee for their work. In this model, the building owner or asset owner contributes 100% of the capital expenditure; he or she keeps 100% of the profits, less management costs. The coworking operator is paid a fixed performance management fee, which typically would be a small percentage of turnover. In this model, the coworking operator makes less money, bears none of the risk and is not required to put forward the capital for the space.

Operating Model C: The third operating model is joint venture. Joint ventures are a hybrid of models A and B. A joint venture typically is between an operator and an asset owner, or it could be between an operator and a large real estate tenant or a corporate. The capital contributions toward the space are shared, anywhere on a scale from 50:50 to 90:10. The ratios are negotiated between the operator and the owner.

The profits derived from the centre are distributed in accordance with the equity, so in a 50/50 scenario the profits are shared equally, less management costs. If the funding is disproportionate, typically the profits are shared disproportionately as well. Under a joint venture model, there's usually a second agreement with the operator which is a management agreement. It's the same agreement as in option B, so the manager is paid a fee for management services and often is performance incentivized as well, as would happen under a management contract. In this environment, the coworking operator and the owner split the risk and the return. The coworking operator typically gets similar or slightly higher return on capital than they would in an owner-operated model because of the economies of scale of working with a partner.

Operating Model D: Finally, the least common model currently in coworking is a franchise model. A franchise model is another hybrid of an owner-operator model with externalised intellectual property and externalised marketing and engagement. Under a franchise model, an aspiring owner-operator, perhaps an asset owner, purchases the IP, marketing brand and sales channels from an existing coworking franchisor and then proceeds to put forward 100% of the capital, bear 100% of the risk and reap 100% of the returns. The risk profile has been lowered because the franchisee is buying into an established brand with established sales and marketing channels. The capital expenditure is slightly higher than a self-funded space because the franchisor has to make the initial franchise purchase of the intellectual property and brand, but the likelihood of success is higher.

With all of these pluses, it seems interesting that the franchise model is so uncommon in coworking. The reason for that is stage of life in the industry; at this stage there are only a few international coworking operators. The coworking operators that are international are currently far more interested in their own expansion and competing for global market share which, at this stage, is a more lucrative endeavour than franchising. However, the franchising model is one I expect to become more common as time goes by.

CHAPTER TWO TAKEAWAYS

▶ Coworking is an incredibly high-touch industry. Operators typically know not only their clients, but each individual employee of those companies.

▶ Successful coworking operators have an understanding of the demographics of the community in their spaces and use that understanding to determine how they construct their business model and therefore solve the needs that are common within that community.

▶ Not all coworking clients are rolling month to month. A significant number of clients across a space will be on six month, twelve month, or even twenty-four or thirty-six-month contracts, which are very similar terms to leases.

▶ The flexibility allowed in coworking actually increases retention as opposed to decreasing it.

▶ Business centres focus on generating the maximum yield per square foot without building a relationship with the client. In coworking spaces, operators look at spend per person; they run on a concept of relational business, which is trust that is developed over time by continued performance and continued delivery.

▶ Coworking spaces operate within a layered economic environment based on location, segmentation (industry), the global and local economies and the coworking space itself (its design, the community within it and the way that it operates).

▶ The most common operating model in the coworking industry right now is an owner-operated model. Alternative models include management contract, joint venture and franchise models.

Chapter Three

TRACING THE TREND – THE GROWTH OF COWORKING

LIGHTING THE FUSE: A GENERATION BURNED

'We'd love to hire you. You are a perfect fit for the role. But the bank has just frozen hiring worldwide and there are thousands of people about to be displaced'. In a few short sentences, the voice on the other end of the phone informed me that my guaranteed graduate job at one of the world's largest banks wasn't going to happen.

I graduated from university in London in 2008 with a first-class honours degree only to enter one of the biggest financial disasters the world had ever seen. Beneath its glass facades, the city of London was silently on fire. In a few months' time, Lehman Brothers would collapse and I would hear stories of formerly highly-paid employees emptying vending machines to clear the credit off their staff cards. The global financial crisis (GFC) had closed virtually every graduate program in the city, making an entire year of graduates practically unemployable.

I was one of the lucky ones. I had several job offers, the best of which offered to pay me 30 percent less than I had been earning while working part-time as a student. I can still remember an interview with *L'Oréal* where I was offered a position on their public relations team if I would work for them for free for a year. I didn't accept either.

A newspaper article at the time claimed that people who graduated in a recession would earn an average of 20 percent less over their lifetimes than people who didn't. There was nothing that could have infuriated me more than the inference that for the rest of my life I would be worth 20 percent less than everybody else. Once people have established a value for themselves in the workplace, it's very uncommon for people to accept a value that is less than that.

I tell this story because I was not alone. Between 2007 and 2010, approximately 8 million people graduated tertiary education in the US, 1.2 million people in the UK and 18 million people across the rest of the European Union. I have come to call these 28 million people[1] who graduated into the worst job market since the great depression 'GFC Graduates.'

Not a lot has been written about this sub-set of Generation Y, but their struggle for employment immediately after a coddled university experience produced a 'sink or swim' micro-generation. They are a group of people with a distrust of big business and big institutions and who have had to fight tooth and nail for everything they have. They are a group of people who were acutely mis-sold the university dream.

To be clear, graduates weren't the only people affected personally by the GFC. In the U.K. total unemployment hit 8.5 percent during the GFC, with youth unemployment hitting 18 percent. Meanwhile, unemployment in the U.S. hit a staggering 10 percent of the working population.[2] This environment has created another very interesting group of people: seasoned professionals with experience and value who were told in no uncertain terms that they were surplus to requirements.

Those that remained, or perhaps I should say survived, in corporate employment through the GFC underwent an equally brutal experience. Some of the bankers I knew at the time would lament their restricted options of employment as, 'Shanghai, Mumbai, Dubai or Good-Bye.' It was a time to shut up, do what you were told and keep your numbers up.

As was the case with me, it is very unpalatable for people to accept a step backwards. The GFC Graduates and the displaced professionals became creative in a bid to maintain their market value. During the financial crisis, traditional employment became riskier than it had ever been and the idea of becoming a freelancer or an entrepreneur and controlling their own destiny less so. Driven by loss of trust in large faceless entities, these people could see their naivety and how they had falsely assumed they were in stable employment. The idea of being employed by themselves and in control of their own risks seemed far less scary than it had ever been in the past.

Many of these graduates and professionals switched into fight or flight mode. After the industries that seemed invincible faltered, guaranteed jobs vanished and good people were told they were no longer valuable in the workplace. The workforce decided to take its destiny into its own hands. In my eyes, the GFC was a catalyst for the current explosion in entrepreneurship.

As I write this book, we are now a decade on from the global financial crisis and we are beginning to see a second wave. Those GFC Graduates are now in their mid-thirties. They are in positions of power and authority in their own businesses and within large organisations they are starting to hold a significant proportion of middle-management positions. With that responsibility, our Gen Y, GFC Graduates are now making buying decisions about where and how they locate their teams in a manner that represents their value sets and their experiences during the GFC. These buyers look for authenticity and a connection with their environment that goes beyond infrastructure. They understand that engagement is worth its weight in gold.

URBAN ORIGINS, EXPLOSIVE GROWTH

Pinpointing the origin of coworking is a contentious topic within the industry. It's challenging because it involves identifying the origin of a movement, not a business. The question is made more difficult when coworking is considered a revival of an instinctive method of collaborative work, reimagined for the modern age. Could anyone really invent something that is innately human? To delve into the chronology of coworking, www.deskmag.com has an excellent published timeline of the most broadly agreed sequence of coworking milestones. I don't intend to argue the nuances of the chronology here, but only to put forward an executive summary one needs to understand the moment.

Coworking first found some fixed infrastructure in 1995 amidst the hacker community when a hackerspace called C-base was launched in Berlin to enable techies to collaborate.[3] By 1999 the word 'coworking' was coined by Brian DeKovan as a way to describe a new type of working where individuals could collaborate, innovate and thrive.

However, it was the period from 2005 to 2006 when the first official 'coworking spaces' opened their doors. Programmer Brad Neuberg opened a non-profit co-op coworking space in San Francisco in 2005 in response to 'unsocial' business centres. The space closed after a year and reopened as a commercial venture known as the Hat Factory in 2006.

The year 2005 also marked the opening of the first Impact Hub in Islington in London. Impact Hub went on to become the first significant franchise operator in coworking and as of 2018 has since grown to over one hundred locations with a presence in more than fifty countries globally.[4] The year 2006 also saw the emergence of Jellies, a critical social component of coworking.

Jellies are organised, collaborative working meet ups where small groups of people come together to collaborate, share ideas and support one another in an informal atmosphere. Therefore, broadly speaking, the coworking industry took the shape we understand today in the period from 2005 to 2006.

After over a decade of growth, at the time of publishing in 2018, there are almost ten coworking environments opening across the world every day. These figures move continuously, but based on the Deskmag 2018 Coworking Forecast - the largest and in my opinion the most representative survey of the industry - there are presently 15,500 coworking environments worldwide with a forecast of 18,900 by the end of 2018. Between 2016 and 2017 the industry grew 43 percent by membership base and this is forecast to continue at 33 percent annual growth through 2018. [5] These are phenomenal levels of expansion by anyone's metrics.

There have been a couple of interesting trends that emerged in the global coworking surveys over the years. The first was in 2016; the average coworking environment had grown its membership by 46 percent. Second, also emerging in the 2016 survey, the biggest coworking environments in the world (by members on average) were located in Asia, a statistic that has remained true through to the present day.

A 2017 study by GCUC (Global Coworking Unconference Conference) and Emergent Research estimates there to be over 4,500 coworking environments in the U.S. at time of print[6] - up from just 14 spaces in 2007. With

638,000 U.S. coworking members, the mean size of a coworking space in the U.S. currently stands at 140 members. It is worth noting, that figure represents a significant increase from the average number of 52 members measured just a few years ago.

Coworking thus far follows commerce and specifically knowledge-based commerce. The cities where coworking is growing exponentially are cities with thriving knowledge-based ecosystems - financial services, technology, consulting - and cities with primarily service-based economies. The same 2017 GCUC and Emergent Research Survey estimates there will be 5.1 million people coworking globally by 2022, supported by an international industry of over 30,000 coworking spaces.

So, what is driving this explosive growth? Some supporting facts and figures are behind the growth of coworking, particularly urban growth. In the Intuit 2020 report published in October 2010, it was projected that by 2020 more than 40 percent of the American workforce, or 16,000,000 people, will be freelance contractors or temp workers. Presently, 28 percent of the Asian workforce is contingent; this figure grew by 10 percent in the past two years. In Singapore specifically, the 2014 Hays Salary Guide states that two-thirds of employers use temporary or contract staff, with 20 percent of them expecting to employ more of such staff over the next twelve months.

At the Global Leadership Summit in London in 2014, 34 percent of business leaders said that more than half of their company's full-time workforce will be working remotely by 2020 and one-quarter of them said that more than three-quarters would be working in a non-traditional office by 2020.

Adam Kingley, the director of Learning Solutions at the London Business School - one of the world's foremost business schools - is quoted as saying flexibility is the number one reason millennials are attracted to a workplace. The Economics Intelligence Unit 2012 Service 2020 report said that by 2020, 55 percent of companies expect they will compete primarily on a service basis, suggesting a drive towards a relational based economy, particularly in urban centres.

The coworking movement has been gathering momentum for some time, has been driven by social trends and is primarily an urban phenomenon.

TIPPING POINT: THE UNEXPECTED SPANISH MARKET

In 2010, Spain had the highest number of coworking environments per capita in Europe. This fact is surprising, given that the makeup of Spain's economy is not one that would be expected to lead the market in coworking, especially when compared with neighboring countries like Germany or the United Kingdom. It's a statistic that became particularly interesting to me when I was trying to explain why, globally in 2010, the coworking industry suddenly began to expand at pace. Spain is interesting because many people deeply associate Spain with the financial crisis, massive youth unemployment and an economy that teetered on the brink of financial ruin.

While those conditions don't sound like the making of an industry, those factors and a few more are exactly why Spain became a center of coworking in Europe when it did, in my opinion. Let's start first with Spain's youthful population. The median age in Spain is just forty-two years old. In fact, over 60 percent of the population falls in between the working ages of fifteen to sixty-four.[7]

When you look at the population pyramid for Spain, you have a shape unlike any other country in Europe, where populations tend to be aging. The peak of the distribution in Spanish population falls between twenty and forty-nine years old. With around 26 percent of the population between the ages of twenty-four and thirty, Spain has a massive Gen Y, the people that were most affected by the global financial crisis.

According to 2014 EU census figures, youth unemployment in Spain for that period was at the highest level in Europe with over 53.5 percent of young Spanish people unemployed. This was double the European average of 23.7 percent for the same period and these figures looked specifically at unemployment of those under twenty-five years of age. [8]

The interesting part about the financial crisis was that while the jobs went away, the work to be done did not. There was still money to be made and things to be done. And when you have a country with a young, idle, educated and arguably frustrated group of people, they find a way to start achieving things. I believe coworking is the way Spanish people found to fight the economic downturn.

In uncertain economic times, one of the easiest ways to find work is to take matters into your own hands and freelance. A boom in Spanish freelancing culture completely explains the boom in Spanish coworking. And when you combine this unprecedented market demand with the unprecedented collapse in Spanish real estate prices, suddenly the concerns of supply and demand in the market have been addressed in a remarkable way.

A snapshot of the Spanish market in 2010 tells us a lot about the factors that trigger explosive growth of coworking in a market. The factors that trigger the perfect storm for coworking growth are:

1. **A large young population**
2. **High youth unemployment**
3. **High percentage of university educated youth**
4. **A historically social culture**
5. **Readily available, well-located rental property at affordable prices.**

In 2010 those factors meant that in Spain, coworking environments could be started by younger people because the cost of entry was lowered, demand was high and the specification of the spaces didn't need to be high to serve the market.

Looking across Europe, the story was repeated city by city as each one entered into a similar state, sparking a chain reaction of coworking growth in London, Paris and Berlin. All experienced high youth unemployment during the global financial crisis. Their property markets all suffered, but in 2010 none of them were in a state quite as extreme as Spain's.

When these factors are looked at, it is actually possible to predict which cities will next experience a coworking boom.

EAST OVERTAKES THE WEST - FIERCE ASIAN GROWTH

Coworking's sustained annual growth rate in excess of 30 percent is massive - it would be for any industry - but when you realise that percentage is a *worldwide* average that includes Africa, rural Europe and rural Asia as well - the significance of that number really begins to sink in. When you look only at Asian cities, the coworking growth rate has been closer to 100% per annum from 2014 to 2018; that trend was mainly driven by spaces in Asian megacitics.

In my home market of Singapore, I witnessed the ferocity of the Asian coworking industry first hand. Singapore closed out 2017 with 750,000 square feet of coworking space. At the end of 2016, it had 200,000 square feet, at the end of 2015 it was at about 100,000 square feet and just 50,000 in the year prior. That's quite an astonishing level of growth. For Singapore, 450,000 square feet is only a small dent in the millions of commercial square feet in Singapore, but when we look at some of the Chinese mega-cities, like Shanghai, we see the trend on an even more macro scale.

In December of 2015, I was invited to speak at the Global Coworking Unconference Conference (GCUC pronounced 'Juicy' by industry insiders) in Shanghai, which was the first GCUC ever in China. Yet in a single event, it became the largest-ever coworking conference in the world, with over 700 attendees - which should offer a hint as to the scale of coworking in China.

Having met hundreds of coworking founders, I can say that when I meet somebody who has a new coworking business, the discussion goes like this: 'Welcome to coworking. How big is your space?' If they are off to a really exciting start, they will reply with an answer between 5,000 or 7,000 square feet. That's a really big space for a new operator, which indicates they're doing quite well. At the GCUC China conference, I met a coworking founder in Shanghai who said, 'You know, I'm new to coworking, we're a startup. We've only been running ten months'. I said, 'Great, how big is your space?' He replied, 'I have fourteen spaces across China, all of them are between 20,000 and 30,000 square feet'. That was my first realisation that coworking in China was a completely different beast when compared to any other market, but particularly comparatively boutique coworking in Europe.

That dramatic growth was driven partly by property ownership in China; large amounts of real estate are still held by private families. It was also driven by high commercial vacancy rates, population size, age, density and the fact that Asia has some of the most expensive real estate prices in the world. All of these are compounding factors that make coworking very appealing within Asian cities.

A NEW WAY OF DOING BUSINESS — PEOPLE LIGHT, REVENUE DENSE BUSINESSES

Throughout this book, I will refer to people light, revenue dense businesses using the acronym PLRD. These businesses are not necessarily small. PLRD is my shorthand for the new generation of business.

Apple is my best example of a PLRD business. It is a surprising example, given that Apple has 123,000 employees. That hardly sounds people light. But in 2017, Apple generated $229.2 billion in revenue. When you divide that figure by the number of its employees, Apple generated $1.8 million per employee. The company's income to employee ratio is astronomical and it sets the gold standard of a PLRD dense business.

Let me put the above example into perspective. An old business coach of mine used to recommend that small businesses turn over at least $100,000 per person. That figure gave them enough money to pay their employees well, pay their bonuses, cover their overheads and make a healthy profit. So, $100,000 per employee is a healthy metric. This represents the difference between the old and new ways of doing business. On the other hand, HSBC, one of the world's largest banks, employs 229,000 people globally. That's 106,000 more people than Apple. The difference between HSBC and Apple is HSBC turns over $225,000 per employee, bringing their annual income to just $51.5 billion by comparison.

Now don't get me wrong, HSBC is a healthy, viable business. It is one of the world's most successful banks and a bank that weathered the financial crisis better than most. But it operates on an old-world economic model. It is people heavy, relative to its income. The company lacks automation and technological advantages and would perform financially comparable to its peers. Apple, by contrast, is peerless. It outperforms other tech companies. It has high turnover and high margins and uses a great deal of automation. Where people are involved, they're delivering intellectual property, they're adding value and they're making their products remarkable.

Today, PLRD businesses are new and emerging, but between 2021 and 2031 it is forecast that the world will experience an unprecedented period of growth led primarily by these types of businesses. The 2031 theorem looks at the technological developments of artificial intelligence, blockchain, virtual reality, drones, 3D printing, quantum computing and robotics all reaching commercial maturity and the potential for businesses to be able to do more with less. In my own business, I've been watching this trend emerge for years.

Collective Works turns over five times the revenue per employee of an older style business, putting it at twice the level of performance to HSBC, albeit not quite in the same league as Apple. My clients are very similar; a huge percentage of coworking customers are people light, revenue dense businesses. They're businesses with a lot of intellectual property and a lot of automation, that highly leverage technology for lean gains and efficiency. The reason that coworking continues to be a fast-growing movement is because we've yet to hit the saturation point.

POWERING THE MOVEMENT — ADVANCEMENT OF TECHNOLOGY AND THE CLOUD

In 2007 a little company called Dropbox was founded. Dropbox was based on the idea of having a little box on the internet that allowed you to access your files from anywhere. Dropbox in my opinion was one of the most influential companies of our time; the company humanised cloud computing and made it accessible to the everyday user. Suddenly, almost everyone I knew had and was using Dropbox, it was so convenient

Also in 2007, Google launched Google Apps Premier Edition. Google Apps offered cloud- hosted email, cloud storage, Google Docs and Spreadsheets and cloud-based calendaring. It was a suite of applications that did away with the need for corporate servers. Users could even access their email on their BlackBerry mobile devices.

So, even in the midst of the financial crisis, technologies were being developed that were fundamentally changing the ways companies and individuals organised their data and managed their information. Google Apps and Dropbox essentially eliminated the need for a physical server inside most companies.

Even at the earliest stage of my coworking business in 2012, 98 percent of my customers used cloud software, 100 percent used some form of cloud email provider and many used cloud productivity software or file storage. For the new PLRD business owner, the cloud was and is the only option that will move fast enough, offer the option to scale indefinitely (without paying for that option) and offer the mobility and redundancy that outperforms most corporates - all in a cost-efficient, pay-as-you-go package.

In my own business, we use cloud email, cloud storage, cloud CRM, cloud accounting, cloud desktop syncing, cloud inventory management, cloud calendaring, a cloud asset management system and cloud archiving and backup. The beauty of this system is that it will scale as we scale - faster and in a more linear fashion than anything we could do ourselves onsite.

For PLRD businesses, being able to tap into the processing power and capabilities that previously only large businesses could afford has brought down so many industry barriers. Access to these new capabilities means that large clients suddenly become within reach. Small teams become more productive and able to punch above their weight. The cloud represents the normalization and democratization of computer systems and technology that used to be prohibitively expensive. The result has been not only an amazing boost to small business, but a critical component to the success of coworking.

Coworking wouldn't exist without the development and normalisation of cloud technologies. These systems have become so ubiquitous now that we almost forget what life was like before smart phones and file-syncing. When you look at the growth of the industry there is an extremely strong correlation between the growth of coworking and the adoption rates for cloud technologies and web-enabled devices like smart phones.

The advancement of cloud technology liberated most traditional businesses from physical, on premise servers.

It gave people the flexibility to live and work in a way that they'd never been able to do previously, when reliant on all hard-wired technology.

THE POP-UP COMPANY — BUSINESS ON A DIFFERENT CLOCK

Developments like Kickstarter and other crowdfunding platforms have also used technology to make raising capital more accessible than ever before. In doing so, they have changed the lifecycle and lifespan of companies. In December of 2010, a small company called Minimal from Chicago, Illinois, raised $942,578 from 13,512 backers in just thirty days through their Kickstarter crowdfunding campaign, exceeding their original funding goal by 6,284%.

The project's goal was to create a watch kit that would convert the then touch screen iPod Nano into a stylish chunky wrist watch. Eighteen months later, an even smaller company called Pebble Technology raised $10,266,845 to create the Pebble E-Paper watch for iPhone and Android, exceeding its funding goal by 10,266% with 68,929 individual backers.

Those two events represent the tipping point of crowdfunding. Both funding initiatives created companies. When it comes to funding, the way the world works has changed: A business doesn't need to be an established industry player to raise life-changing amounts of money and bring its vision to market. The market is now able to decide if it thinks an idea is worthy of production, preventing great ideas from being left on the cutting room floor and ultimately creating an environment where business ideas have more potential to grow than ever before.

Beyond the relative ease of launching new technologically-enabled business ideas, these developments in technology are a signifier of something else going on in the world: We already have all the big companies we will ever need to cater to our manufacturing requirements. There is no product that can't already be produced by the manufacturing technology that is available today (and if there is, the world's existing manufacturers will race to solve this problem). For new companies, it doesn't make sense to enter such a crowded market and it is far more efficient and cost effective to outsource these activities to the developing world.

Instead of the continuation of a manufacturing-based economy, the evolution of computer technology has triggered the rise of the knowledge-based economy. The developed world needs thinkers, creatives and problem solvers who can leverage the technology available today to respond to the market's needs and solve future problems. The concept of coworking is one example of a relevant success story.

Businesses that were created out of ecosystems like Kickstarter and that start and end their lives online, expand and contract at a pace of which we haven't seen previously. My earlier example of Pebble was a much-loved company that went on to last just three years in business before it filed for insolvency and was acquired by smart device maker Fitbit. Businesses today need exist for only as long as they are required and they vanish as quickly as they are created. Very much like the gig economy, the advancement of technology has meant business can now be transient and transactional.

CHAPTER THREE TAKEAWAYS

▶ As a result of the 2008 Global Financial Crisis, many of the 28 million people who graduated into the worst job market since the great depression took matters into their own hands by starting their own businesses, serving as a catalyst for the current explosion in entrepreneurship.

▶ In 2019, those 'GFC Graduates' are in their mid-thirties and are in positions of power and authority in their own businesses and within large organisations. They are now making buying decisions about where and how they locate their teams in a manner that represents their value sets and their experiences during the GFC. These buyers look for authenticity and a connection with their environment that goes beyond infrastructure.

▶ Coworking thus far follows knowledge-based commerce. The cities where coworking is growing exponentially are cities with thriving knowledge-based ecosystems - financial services, technology, consulting - and cities with primarily service-based economies.

▶ With Spain's incredibly high youth unemployment rate and collapse in Spanish real estate prices, came a boom in Spanish freelancing culture and therefore Spanish coworking.

▶ The fierce growth of coworking in Asian countries is driven by population size, density and the fact that Asia has some of the most expensive real estate prices in the world. All of these are compounding factors that make coworking very appealing within Asian cities.

▶ A business trend towards people light, revenue dense (PLRD) businesses will contribute to a growth in coworking. PLRD businesses have a lot of intellectual property and a lot of automation that highly leverage technology for lean gains and efficiency.

WHAT COWORKING SHOULD BE – APPLYING THE COWORKING METHODOLOGY

Based on my experience and empirical research, I'd like to propose a new definition of coworking – one that will form the foundation for the ideas to come throughout the rest of this book. In my theory of the coworking methodology, for an environment to be considered a coworking environment, it must:

- Have an expressed mission to enable and empower
- Foster connection and community by curating an exclusive network
- Be effective
- Be efficient
- Be flexible
- Have a positive impact

MISSION DRIVEN

The most important aspect of the coworking methodology is to define a mission. Coworking is more than a venue. It's only possible to build community around purpose, therefore, it's incredibly important to have a function or a reason for being. By having a mission, a coworking environment will attract people that are best suited to work there. That means that the community thus formed will be more focused. The members of those communities will be more relevant to each other and provide more value, creating a community that's healthier and will endure.

With the flexible structure of coworking, people can choose to subscribe to a month-to-month membership. Therefore, they can continually choose to stay at a coworking environment, or not. They have the option to leave at almost any point, so they will only stay as long as the space continues to provide value to them. One of the best ways to provide value is to be more relevant to them than any other space can be.

In my travels, I have seen dozens of other reasons for starting a coworking environment, all of which were wrong. I know of a coworking environment that was opened for the purpose of giving the owner a platform for academic discussion. It failed. I have seen coworking environments open as feeder businesses to law firms and corporate services companies; they also were not successful. The model I most detested was the coworking environment that was opened by a serviced office provider as a refit of an underperforming serviced office in a vain attempt to rally that underperforming asset. The latter example treated their members with such disdain that the provider ruined their reputation in the local market and were forced to shift their focus elsewhere in Asia while their brand recovered.

The mission behind a coworking environment becomes the theme, the feel, the taste and the smell that runs throughout the entire business. If those qualities present negatively in a relational business such as coworking, then they permeate your entire environment like a toxic corporate culture. Imagine for a minute my final example, a mission to rally an underperforming asset: clients become P&L fodder and concern for wellbeing is replaced by concern for yield because the space is already underperforming. This means there will be no little touches and no personal approach; members are treated like lines on a spreadsheet.

The only reason to create a coworking environment, in my opinion, is to empower the operator's target client. If the coworking environment delights and engages its members and helps them on a journey, the operator will be rewarded and their business will be successful.

COLLABORATIVE AND EXCLUSIVE

It is important for a coworking environment to foster collaboration and community. The first part of that function is creating an exclusive network. The other part is to establish a duty of care or a duty of responsibility over the coworking environment, or to essentially be a host.

As a venue - an environment where these companies are coming to work - somebody has to be in charge and responsible for initiating what needs to be done. Everybody in the space is busy working on their daily business; it is the responsibility of the coworking environment to organize opportunities for collaboration, community building and networking.

Within coworking environments, there has been an evolution of the term 'community manager' or 'space host.' At Collective Works, we have a department we call Engagement. We don't have just one person, we have a group of people that are responsible for looking at how we continually engage our communities. The department looks at social media, events and regular touch points of engagement.

Every Friday in our spaces, we have what we call Friday Treat. My team loads up a hostess trolley and wheels it around the space with a little snack - a cupcake, a glass of wine or a themed seasonal surprise - at around 3 p.m. My team loves participating in this practice and posing for selfies with members; we use it as a chance to speak to every single person in the space once a week. At our core, people are social. As a community, we have to maintain contact with each other for us to actually be a community, not simply a collection of various people.

RELIGION, POLITICS AND THE BUSINESS OF TRIBES

When I was getting started with Collective Works, I worked with a talented small contractor, who I will call Michelle. Michelle is a multi-lingual, western-educated Singaporean with a strong design eye. The reason we got on so well is that we speak a common design language. She can understand design nuances immediately, such as why a light switch needs to be moved thirty centimetres to the left, or why a bracket needs to be removed and refitted so it can't be seen.

After working together on a number of projects and having met her charming husband, I discovered that she and her husband are Jehovah's Witnesses. While this fact didn't faze me, it is an interesting piece of information for a reason I am about to explain.

Some months later, Michelle brought a good friend of hers to Collective Works to have a look around the space as a potential office. Unbeknownst to her, I had met this gentleman previously at the launch of the Rolls Royce Wraith. I knew he was a heavy hitter before she'd given me any background information and I knew he worked in finance. I learned over the course of our conversation that he had worked in a private bank and had left to build a new software platform to change the way hedge funds do business.

Curious about the connection she had with someone who seemed to come from such a different industry, I asked Michelle, 'How did you get to know such an interesting individual?'

She didn't miss a beat, 'We go to the same church.'

It was a short sentence, but it was a complete answer. That short phrase was imbued with so much meaning. It could instantly explain something as complex as why a small interior renovations business owner would know the intricacies of the life and business of a captain of an industry in a completely disparate field.

That is why the fact that she is a Jehovah's Witness is an interesting piece of information. What I instantly understood was that she was part of a clearly defined tribe, or community.

A community is a group of people who are relevant, proximate, engaged and connected through a common axis. The most important element of a community is the axis; for my contractor and this friend of hers, that axis was their religion.

Being part of the right community leads to increased capabilities and opportunities. Look at the emphasis some of the world's highest performing companies place on corporate culture and how vigorously they search for employees of the right 'fit.' Or look at the spontaneous communities of crowdfunding or mass rallies; when people organize themselves rapidly around a common goal, amazing things can happen at an accelerated pace. Furthermore, the economies they create are beneficial for all involved.

Communities are made up of people who share a personal connection - they can be your friends and the friends of your friends, but they can also be bonded to you in a different way. While there might only be six degrees of separation between you and everyone else on the planet - and we now have LinkedIn to tell us just how you are connected to each person - the first two degrees of separation are the most important. Beyond two connections, the relationship becomes abstract, the friend of a friend of a friend. This means the connection loses credibility. Credible connections form communities, meaning they consist of first, second and occasionally third-degree connections. Anything beyond third-degree connections is just a network.

People who strongly identify with any clearly defined belief structure, be it religion, politics, company values or even something as diffuse as an alumni association or professional body, are at a unique advantage within those groups when compared to people with no affiliations.

I will run with the church metaphor to keep it relevant to the story. If you and I go to the same church it means first and foremost that we have the same belief structure. We are governed by the same rules and code of conduct, we believe in the same outcomes and we have a common perspective on the world.

It also means we share a community. This is quite powerful because you aren't just known by a random collection of people I also know. You are known by a group of people I actively choose to be a part of, who I value and who value me. There is implicit acceptance by being part of a strongly-defined community.

Sharing a community also means that it is very easy for me to background check you. Anyone in business can do the standard checks: bankruptcy, litigation and director profiles. However, if I am part of the same community I will find out if you cheat on your spouse, if your tax history is slightly grey or if you have a drinking problem. If these conditions have not escalated to the degree where they have legal or criminal history, I may never hear of them otherwise. But by being part of the same community, my respected, qualified peers will give me a very honest assessment of both your personal and professional history.

There is also a second layer of protection to being part of the same community: Because you are known, you are also held immediately accountable. If we go into business together and you misbehave, then I have recourse. Legal action pales in comparison to the social shame (not to mention religious damnation) of cheating your business partner from the same church. The threat of losing your tribe is so powerful it keeps people on their best behaviour. Communities, in essence, are therefore self-governing; they decide if you make the cut.

The catch is that communities must be supported by infrastructure. They need urban planning or some common ground on which to operate. In large corporations, company offices or a corporate campus serve that purpose. In a church, the physical church and events run by the church form that infrastructure. In housing estates, you find co-op boards; in country clubs, you find membership communities. Those who play together, stay together.

In today's world, we no longer live in small communities. In fact, more and more of us live internationally, thousands of miles away from the places of our birth and from the communities we grew up within. The challenge becomes, in today's increasingly disparate and mixed up world, how do we find communities that allow us to function at the levels of authenticity that we had years ago?

Large companies, historically, have had departments like human resources, corporate affairs and even place management that serve that purpose, but today, even large companies don't consolidate their employees in single locations. More and more, companies are opening branch offices in far-away places, on different continents and in different times zones. Maintaining a sense of community remotely has become increasingly challenging.

This is where collaborative work environments come into play. The best coworking environments are focused, selective and even exclusive: They have a sense of a common culture. They have a rule book. They have a co-op board. What that means is, they have standards and a very clearly defined target audience. In other words, coworking environments consist of tribes. There are ways to create and protect culture when companies are sending employees far away from home.

If you choose to work with a space that aligns with your values, it means you've joined a collective. You've found a new community, a community away from home. For me, this component was incredibly critical in my own personal life, as well as an impetus for creating a coworking business.

EFFECTIVE

The next criterium for a coworking environment is for it to be effective. It must enable the user and align with the mission of the space. There are two steps to doing this. First, equipping members with the tools that they need and second, reducing complexity around using them. These steps need to be done together.

When I was younger, I used to have painting lessons from a lovely man called Ahmed Mansoori. He was a calm and gentle man, a professional watercolour painter who enjoyed passing his skills on. Whenever my parents would ask him what brushes or paints to buy me, he would say, 'Buy the best. How can you expect your son to be the best painter without the best tools?' So, I had great brushes and great paints and for a young child at least I was a pretty great painter.

The same goes for a coworking environment. How can a coworking environment enable its users without providing them with the right tools? Coworking environments have a duty to provide their users with the best quality equipment and tools that they can for the purpose they have outlined.

This isn't to say that coworking environments should continually splurge on upgrades and buy the next big thing as soon as it comes out. Empowering PLRD business leaders means spending on what will have the biggest impact on their experience of the space. In coworking, this is usually technology and IT infrastructure.

(There are very few things more important to modern business leaders than the Internet.)

Essentially, being effective means the space has to work. Coworking operators become the backbone of somebody's business. They're the client's internet connection, their power, their utilities, their workspace. If the they don't create an environment that is effective, then it has a negative impact on the productivity of not just on one, but on the many businesses that share the space. Coworking is quite a privileged platform because the inverse is also true and when an operator does well, their community allows them to amplify that success.

EFFICIENT

Efficiency and its partner philosophy, the reduction of waste, should be core tenets of any business in the modern world. Waste and inefficiency are equally abhorrent; they have no place in business. Thankfully, the coworking movement goes a long way towards addressing these issues in every aspect of its execution.

A chunk of the profit margin of coworking is in the exploitation of the inefficiencies in traditional office planning. Global workspace utilisation surveys indicate that the best offices in the world, with the highest level of utilisation, trend between 60 to 70 percent utilisation. This means that any given day, only 60 to 70 percent of the desks provided will be in use.

In other words, the best and most efficient multi-national corporations worldwide are wasting between 30 to 40 percent of their office real estate. While that's bad enough, remember those are the best planned offices, but in Singapore I have heard of large commercial real estate portfolios running at closer to 40 percent utilisation. With coworking environments, we know we can bring that figure closer to 90 percent utilisation.

Profitability is sustainability. If an operator wants to keep a business in motion and continue to provide a service, it must continue to make a profit. It's important that coworking environments are efficient in how they design, operate and run their spaces, because they're the backbone of dozens if not hundreds of businesses; their footprint is their clients' footprint.

At Collective Works, we use only A-star energy-rated appliances and A-star water-rated appliances and all of the lighting that we install is LED or energy efficient. Yes, we want to minimize our utility bills, but we also recognize that we should be building coworking environments to last ten or twenty years. To do so, we should be building them using the best technologies that are available at the current point in time. We should be building them in a way that enables efficiency and a sustainable approach for the companies in residence, due to the cascading impact of what we do.

FLEXIBLE

More than ever, flexibility in life and in business is something that is being sought after. In buildings, plasticity is the holy-grail of building management and something that has been nearly impossible to achieve. The only aspect of flexibility that is surprising is how little of it we all tend to enjoy in our everyday lives. People are flexible by nature and becoming more so has been enabled by technology.

In terms of running a business, however, flexibility can be seen as counterintuitive: Why would a business owner want to allow their clients to come and go as they please when what most businesses strive for is recurring revenue? One fundamental shift coworking delivered was the change from a leasing model to a membership or subscription model. Flexibility can actually be an attraction and retention tool. People join because they know they aren't overcommitting and they stay because they know they won't get such flexibility under other circumstances. It's a win-win for treating members as people.

Flexibility is also linked to a coworking space's mission and collaborative environment. As people grow and change they may outgrow the mission of the space, so it may be in their best interest to find a new community better suited to their needs. In terms of maintaining a focused community, it's also important to the manager to maintain flexibility so that they can continue to refine the environment they operate.

THE FRAMEWORK FOR COMMUNITY

In an effective community both the Hardware (the physicality) and Software (the rituals and practices) need to align with the global mission of the space. That alignment around a mission sits at the core of community and engagement activity it is the on-mission activity that wraps around both. Engagement is the operating approach that reinforces the social elements - It's living the values in every aspect of the business.

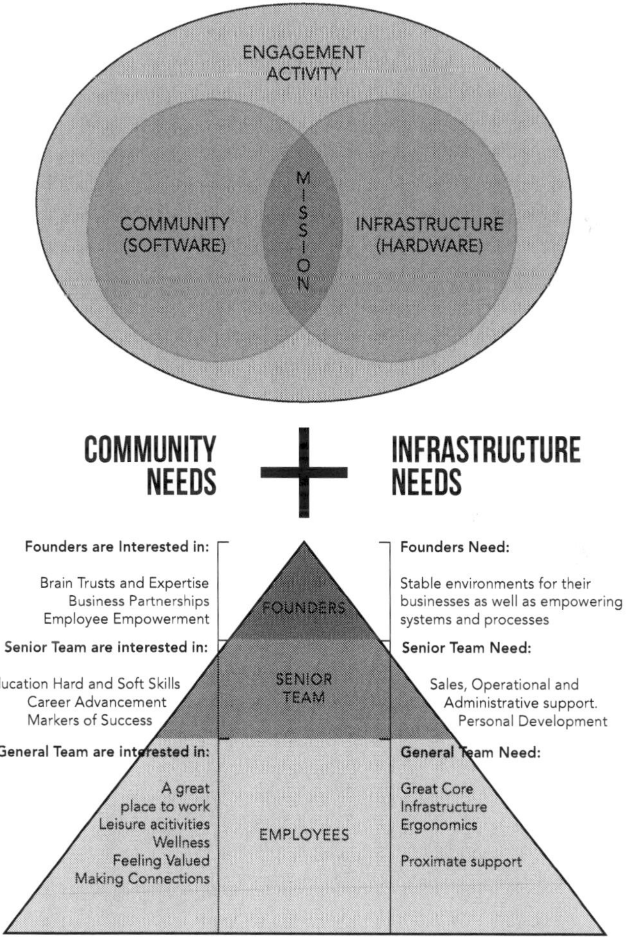

For a working community to succeed, it needs to acknowledge and cater to the different needs of its members at their different professional stages. The Pyramid represents the typical coworking community composition by professional seniority: a small number of Founders, a few more Senior Team and a much greater number of General Team members.

In coworking, the framework of a community involves three key components: infrastructure, community and engagement.

Infrastructure is what a community depends on to operate. The infrastructure of a community is incredibly important; it's something that needs to be built well from the start, so that the community is set up for success. If the infrastructure of a community is flawed, it can create huge problems going forward in terms of the longevity of the community. In a coworking or office environment, infrastructure includes the physical space, services, connectivity to the internet, phones, the quality of the wifi, the quality of the ergonomic chairs and the level of comfort - everything that can be seen, touched, felt and smelled within the physical environment.

Community and cohesiveness refers to an emotional sense of belonging or sense of community; it is the soft factor to a space. The mistake a lot of large corporations make is to think that engagement happens just by putting people in the same space. This is the misnomer behind the idea of the corporate headquarters; if you construct a structure that represents for your brand - a Googleplex, Microsoft campus or Apple Park for example - that alone doesn't mean the space offers a sense of engagement.

Employees and team members can be disengaged even in the most beautiful environments. It helps to have such a structure, because capturing the company's philosophy and ideology in the physical environment acts to under-score the elements of its ethos. Apple's campus, as an example, has a 100,000-square-foot wellness centre and miles of walking trails through orchards and gardens. This design shows a company commitment to wellness and mindfulness. However, unless the culture actively encourages people to go for walks or to use the wellness centre, then the infrastructure goes underutilised, discontentment is created and the community becomes disengaged. Systems, processes, methodologies and traditions have to be created around the physical infrastructure that drive engagement.

Therefore, the third component of a community is engagement. These processes and traditions - the Friday drinks, the Monday morning croissants, the Wednesday afternoon walking meetings - have to be managed on an ongoing basis. Someone has to continually work to generate that warmth, wellness and sense of belonging to ensure that these traditions are kept alive. In a coworking environment, the operator takes a really important role in the engagement of both the infrastructure and the engagement.

All three of these elements have to be present in sufficient quantity and quality to create a truly engaged and contented community. When all of them work in synergy - fantastic infrastructure, high engagement and fluid management - an incredibly successful and powerful working environment can be created.

CHAPTER FOUR TAKEAWAYS

▶ A clear mission will attract companies that are best suited to a given coworking space thereby making its members more relevant to each other. This in turn provides more value and creates a community that's healthier and more enduring.

▶ A coworking environment should foster collaboration and community. The first part of that function is creating an exclusive network. The other part is to establish a duty of care over the coworking environment.

▶ A coworking environment must enable the user. There are two steps to doing this. First, equipping members with the tools that they need and second, reducing complexity around using them. These steps need to be done in tandem.

▶ Efficiency and the reduction of waste should be core tenants of any business. The coworking environment goes a long way towards addressing these issues in every aspect of its execution.

▶ In coworking, the framework of a community involves three key components: infrastructure, engagement and management.

OUR DYSFUNCTIONAL RELATIONSHIP WITH REAL ESTATE

Leasing and real estate structures are primed for disruption. The way that people buy and rent real estate hasn't changed for hundreds of years: long-term leases, fixed rental costs and a structure of very low value exchange. Real estate, as currently structured, offers little to no relationship among parties. It doesn't match the way the world now moves and it doesn't align with current-day business culture.

Real estate as a concept has been designed to prioritise the landlord, or landowner, at the expense of the tenant. What we're seeing in the coworking industry now is the very beginnings of a broad dissatisfaction with our relationship with our physical environment. We need to move beyond an asset-focused mentality. We need to look at relationships. We need to look at individuals and start bridging the divide between our physical environments and our ideological selves.

VOLATILE LEASING COSTS

If you work in commercial real estate, no one has to tell you that the last decade or so has been a colourful one. From the boom times of 2005 and 2006, to the collapse in real estate prices in 2007 and 2008 and through the 'road to recovery' this decade has not been for the faint of heart.

In Manhattan, the price of office rent ranges from $20 to more than $100 per square foot per annum, depending on location, proximity to transportation, amenities offered in the building and the age of the building. In 2016, the average price per square foot of office space topped the 2008 high of $100 to hit $110. While demand for office space in New York City has declined over the past decade, it is projected that demand will overtake supply by 2020. [9]

In London, the commercial real estate market is approximately half the size of the New York City market. While London was hit hard by the economic downturn, today office vacancy rates are at their pre-downturn levels of just 4.5 percent and average office rents have topped their 2007 high of £115 to hit £120 per square foot.

Meanwhile, Singapore, with more than eighty million square feet of office space, is the fourth most expensive commercial real estate market in Asia, behind Beijing,

Tokyo and Hong Kong. In 2014, office vacancy rates were at 4 percent, their lowest since the economic downturn, while the average office rent per square foot for grade A property has stayed fairly steady since 2009 at about $138 per square foot per annum.

In a world with a human population of over seven billion that is growing at a rate of 1.1 percent per year, it is certain that things are going to get more crowded. We need to think more creatively about our physical environment and our utilisation of it. Do we still live in a world where it is viable to have office buildings occupied only during the day and hotels occupied only at night? Will we need to reconsider the applications of our buildings and our relationship to them?

INSTABILITY A NEW NORMAL

If we learned anything over the last decade it is that real estate now follows the stock market. What that means is that businesses are less able to forecast their headcount needs in different markets and it is harder for them to make long-lead decisions such as commitments to real estate.

In 2017, I went to hear the British economist Jeremy Cook speak on the impact of Brexit and the U.S. election of President Trump. On stage he said, 'The first thing that people ask me, knowing I'm a British economist is, "Brexit. Really?" And then they ask, "What does it mean?" I reply, "The scary thing is, we don't know."' This is just the most recent consideration.

We've had ten years of instability since the global financial crisis. Now, we've got Brexit pending and Donald Trump as U.S. President and no one knows what that is going to do to the global markets. What's going to happen with international trade? What's that going to do to real estate prices or head count in different parts of the world? Nobody knows at this stage, because the situation is unprecedented and creates so many variables.

Add to those factors the challenge of creating spaces that remain relevant to changing workforce demographics, advancing technology and business dynamics. With a workforce that comprises Baby Boomers all the way through to Generation Z, creating a work environment that suits such a spectrum is quite a challenge; it's costly to achieve, especially as companies become increasingly decentralised. Catering spaces to that diverse of a workforce is becoming even harder, when companies don't have the critical mass of centralised real estate that they used to.

HUMAN SCALE VERSUS ENGINEERING SCALE

Buildings are designed by engineers. Engineers like to design spaces that are large, regular, have low ceilings, have a homogenous layout and that are efficient. Engineers design buildings this way to maximise usable floor plate and energy efficiency. Typically, they design buildings for large single occupants or large tenants.

Now here's the challenge. While designing for energy efficiency and designing for single occupants is a great idea on paper, in practice buildings are rarely used that way. What makes matters worse is that users don't like the same kind of spaces that engineers do. People prefer intimate spaces, spaces that don't have, say, more than 100 people in them. They prefer spaces with natural light, spaces that feel spacious and that have high ceilings. Many people like spaces that are irregular or contain artefacts or unique elements like heritage buildings.

Unfortunately, a lot of these characteristics that make spaces comfortable for people create problems from an engineering standpoint. High ceilings, for example, increase heating and cooling costs. For spaces to be small enough that people feel comfortable, engineers must design multi-story buildings, which causes operational inefficiencies for large companies that therefore have to be divided among multiple floors.

Commercial real estate is faced with a challenge: New buildings are typically built by engineers for large corporate tenants. Older buildings in cities tend to be seen now as too small or too inefficient, too quirky, or too irregular to be used by corporate clients. But in today's world, there are companies that are both big and small. There are big companies that have small offices and small branches, innovation teams and remote teams, or that are even segmented within themselves into smaller departments or sections. There are small companies that make a lot of money and can afford lovely spaces but don't want inefficiency, or that have a global presence.

Our current approach to real estate lacks a system to get the physical environment to interface with the way that companies operate and the way that companies plan their spaces. If the coworking methodology is applied, it gives landlords a system with a 'software layer' that allows them to simultaneously place a single occupant (a coworking operator) and multiple occupants (the coworking members) in the same space. Coworking therefore acts as a bridge between a number of buildings. It has been evidenced that the coworking methodology works when applied to a large floor plate, to new purpose-built office blocks, as well as to quirky heritage buildings which typically have gone unused for a considerable period of time.

In many ways, the coworking methodology works as the bridge between human scale and engineering scale, giving each the best of both worlds in terms of operational efficiency and human experience.

LACK OF SUSTAINABILITY

When we look at the future of coworking, with an increased operating scale and increased number of businesses being catered to, the need for sustainability increases exponentially. Operating spaces with large margins put a cost pressure on sustainability. There is also a greater responsibility; when a coworking business takes over providing workspace for dozens if not hundreds of companies, the coworking business's footprint is effectively the carbon footprint of the businesses being looked after. That in itself is a sobering thought.

The great news is that coworking, fundamentally, is a lot more sustainable than building a company's own office. In a traditional real estate transaction, commercial space is rented bare; typically, it has a finished floor and perhaps a false ceiling, maybe light fittings. In some cases, the space is only concrete slabs, walls and windows. I've seen offices in Singapore where companies even have to install their own air conditioning.

The sustainability challenge is that a typical commercial lease is for two to three years, with a two- or three-year renewal; a very large corporation could negotiate a ten- or twenty-year lease. After the two- to three-year window, the space is effectively gutted. A perfectly usable fit is thrown away. Then the cycle repeats. The constant cycle of construction and demolition of interior renovations and the discarding of perfectly serviceable interiors and fits is grossly unsustainable.

I was shown the 30,000-square-foot offices of a very famous social network in Singapore after they vacated it and moved into a new building. They had left behind probably five or six million dollars in fit, including electric sit/stand desks and ergonomic furniture. The furniture and the fit were left there for anybody who wanted it, but if nobody wanted it, it was going to be thrown away.

Looking at the sustainability profile of the way businesses have run offices to date is appalling. Coworking, alternatively, provides a space that can be reused and recycled and used by many generations of companies as they scale and exit and a new generation starts. Coworking is far more sustainable than a build-your-own profile. On top of that, when operating hours are looked at, with many spaces operating 24/7 there is a lot of pressure on making sure operators use sustainable building services.

NEEDLESS DUPLICATION

Another challenge facing decentralised offices is the issue of wasted resources. Decentralised offices, unfortunately, are hugely wasteful in isolation. Imagine the needs of 100 decentralised offices. One hundred decentralised offices will require 100 phones lines, 100 internet connections, 100 printers, 100 electricity bills, 100 modems, 100 rental leases, 100 reception areas, 100 kettles, 100 coffee machines and 100 countless other resources. This scenario creates an enormous amount of duplication. Where there is duplication there is inefficiency and where there is inefficiency there is waste.

By contrast, in a company with 500 staff members, all of those people will have access to the same infrastructure – the same phone line, internet connection, printers, electricity, modem, rental lease, reception area, kettles, coffee machines and more. First, this lowers the cost per user. Second, it also means that this infrastructure is in frequent use, thus reducing the amount of downtime where resources simply cost money without providing any return.

DECENTRALISED BUSINESS AND MEGA REAL ESTATE – THE TRILLION-DOLLAR ISSUE

When a large company considers the under-utilisation and overspending of their real estate across large portfolios, they realise the need for a different real estate model. Historically, companies chose to offshore when driven by economic reasons but experience has shown offshoring is not a like-for-like replacement. There are functions of a business that would benefit from an enriched environment - one where their people can experience a new working culture of innovation.

Decentralizing businesses is saving companies worldwide hundreds of millions of dollars a year. There are case studies of HSBC in Hong Kong as well as Cisco Systems and Microsoft globally decentralizing their teams. Even traditional businesses, such as large consumer banks, are jumping on this trend by moving functions out of major cities and into low-cost real estate markets and downsizing their CBD (Central Business District) headquarters.

These large businesses are looking at operators like coworking environments that offer them space in the CBD at a 30 percent discount over what they were paying. In New York, for example, where a desk in a multinational office typically costs an organisation $10,000 a year, major coworking operators will be able to provide an equivalent desk in an equivalent location for $7,000 a year. With little further complexity, that in itself represents a 30 percent savings even on a one-to-one replacement basis with no loss of quality and perhaps even an improvement to the employee experience of being part of an engaging, exciting environment.

For the first time in the history of corporate real estate, the opportunity to decentralize and reduce real estate costs is also paired with an opportunity to improve the workspace experience of the people that work for large organisations. An employee of a large organisation in charge of servicing or delivering new products to customers now has the opportunity to get closer to the clients that they're working for. The employee could go to networking drinks with clients and learn in depth how they feel about their product in a way that they never could while trapped in their corporate headquarters.

CASE STUDY – A BANK WITH SINGAPORE OPERATIONS

In today's fast-paced business landscape, the ability for large corporations to predict the future and accurately plan for their expansion needs and requirements with physical real estate has rapidly diminished. The challenge for these massive real estate consumers is that their real estate decisions operate in the territory of tens - if not hundreds - of millions of dollars. An incorrect decision has a huge impact to profitability and bottom line.

Here's a prime example: A financial institution in Singapore recently subleased three floors from a competing bank in a neighbouring highrise tower because they suddenly required extra real estate. That in itself is unusual, but the surprising piece of information is that eighteen months earlier, that same bank had written off what I estimate to be fifty million dollars of commercially fitted-out space in their building and returned five floors to the landlord of the precinct. As a result of that decision, they're now in a situation where they're paying a higher-rate lease on space that is not even in the same building that they occupy and they had to write-down undepreciated fitout. They couldn't see eighteen months ahead of themselves at the point in which they were making their real estate decisions.

Can a bank absorb a loss-making manoeuvre like that? It can, but it shouldn't have to - and neither should the environment, since scrapping and re-fitting a completely serviceable space like that leaves a negative ecological footprint as well. Unfortunately, this scenario has become so much more of a reality for large corporations than it ever used to be. The idea of building a corporate headquarters and working in it for twenty years is gone.

However, the soon-to-be-attainable solution for these large operators is the idea of a business, or a building, that can expand and contract with the company's needs. Imagine that this financial institution could expand and assume two floors in a building if needed and then contract and lose that overhead when they don't need the space. With a business environment that is becoming less predictable and less profitable as our global markets mature, the need to be more dynamic in business, in a sustainable way, is increasing.

This dynamism can be fuelled by coworking. Envision a building as a sandwich with an expandable, compressible coworking layer in the middle. This model can support rapid expansions and contractions within the building. When considering the future of business, companies will want to work in buildings which are sustainable and which cater to the needs of modern, multi-national companies and also offer flexible expansion space. Large tenants should not be forced to pay a premium for the volatile natures of the markets and the world we now live in.

CHAPTER FIVE TAKEAWAYS

- ▶ Global markets, international trade and real estate prices in different parts of the world are becoming even more unpredictable. Thus, businesses are less able to forecast their headcount needs in different markets and it is harder for them to make long-lead decisions, such as commitments to real estate.

- ▶ Businesses face the challenge of creating spaces that remain relevant to a changing workforce demographic, from Gen Y all the way through to Baby Boomers. The coworking methodology can be a solution to all of the aforementioned challenges.

▶ In many ways, the coworking methodology works as the bridge between human scale and engineering scale, giving each the best of both worlds in terms of operational efficiency and human experience.

▶ Coworking is far more sustainable than a build-your-own profile. It provides a space that can be reused and recycled and used by many generations of companies as they scale and exit and a new generation starts.

▶ Decentralizing businesses is saving companies worldwide hundreds of millions of dollars a year. Large businesses are looking at operators like coworking environments to provide a discount over what they were paying. Even traditional businesses are jumping on this trend by moving functions out of major cities and into low-cost real estate markets and downsizing their CBD (Central Business District) headquarters.

WHO COWORKING IS FOR

Coworking originally started as a movement around office sharing shortly after it formalised into a service provider/client relationship . Nowadays, we've seen coworking evolve into multinational businesses with the advent of operators such as WeWork. However, even with major operators, coworking still only accounts for perhaps 2 percent of CBD real estate in cities like New York. The reality is (and will continue to be) that the majority of commercial real estate is leased by corporations. That's not necessarily a bad thing and that doesn't mean that coworking isn't going to proliferate.

As the coworking model proves itself and as the model matures, corporate lessors of space will start to apply the coworking methodology to their own businesses. They will start to change the way that they look at the segmentation of space, or change the way they plan their real estate. They will no longer adopt a full-time equivalent,

THE EXPANDING TARGET DEMOGRAPHIC OF COWORKING

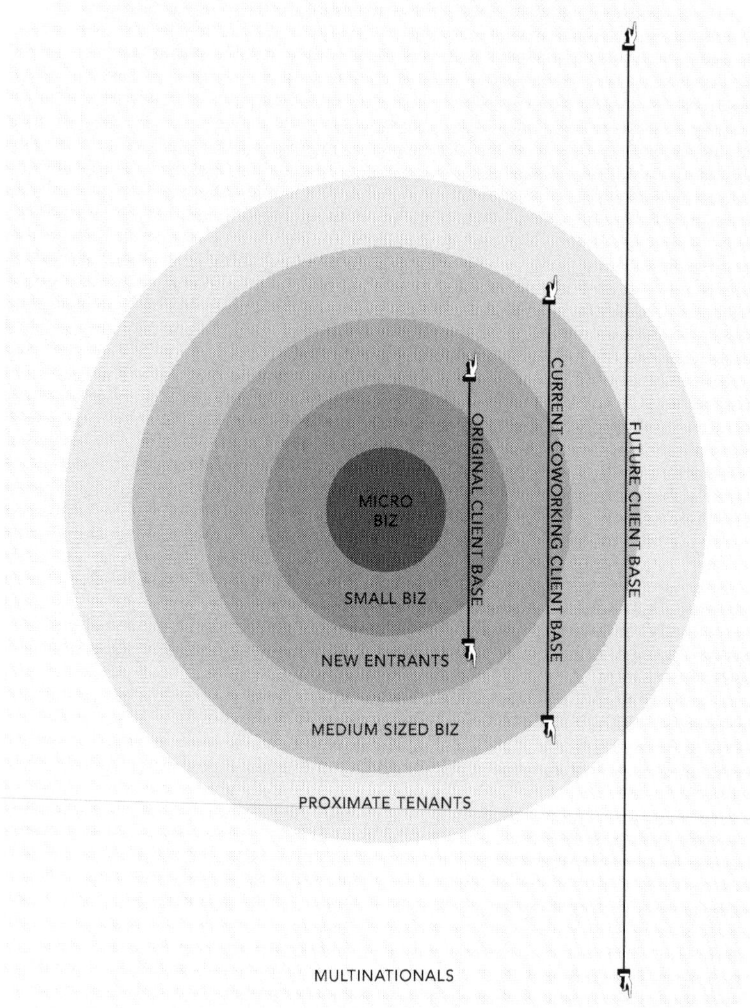

five-year advance planning model and instead look to plan real estate in percentages of fixed space and percentages of flexed space. From an operating perspective, it will make more sense to pay a running premium on flexible space than it will to carry vacancy or to continually fit, rip and repeat.

Coworking is a method that can be applied in a number of different ways to different markets and with different needs. The origins of coworking may have begun with small businesses, but very quickly large corporate real estate consumers realised that the benefits of the coworking methodology could be applied to their businesses as well as part of the corporate real estate portfolio mix.

A corporation would have to go through a decision matrix in terms of planning what areas of their business could make use of coworking – namely which areas are fixed versus flex. Some departments cannot be outsourced; compliance or data security, or even a company's internal IT department, will always need to be part of HQ. But other departments which have different technological requirements could be decentralised. A bank, for example, could eliminate all of its branches. There's no need for banks to have all of those spaces as they could be collocated with their customers.

Banks are an interesting example to stay with because retail banking in particular experiences some unusual legacy real estate choices. Bank branches, for example, are generally located in high value ground floor retail locations, but they experience low utilisation with very poor foot traffic. They exist because they are the legacy of retail banking, but a clear opportunity exists to move these branches closer to customers in a way that could add more value and significantly reduce real estate spend by micronizing their branch network into collocated workspaces.

Banks also typically have significant marketing, customer service and sales departments. These could also be moved into flex space, because they're roving and they could benefit from client interaction. It's also preferable to consolidate these teams into coworking spaces versus offering home-based working, due to regulatory and compliance as well as issues of poor engagement and productivity associated with home-working.

PLRD DIFFUSE TEAMS + ENTREPRENEURS

People Light Revenue Dense businesses and entrepreneurs are really the genesis market of coworking. They are interesting because they tend to expand internationally at a much smaller size than companies of old. Because of this tendency, PLRD businesses can end up with a matrix of people spread globally and so require a diffuse infrastructure to support them. In these businesses a snapshot can be seen of how a global business could be structured without the burden of legacy.

Because of their relative sophistication, PLRD businesses need many of the same facilities as big businesses, but in this diffuse format PLRD remote teams lack the purchasing power to access them. PLRD remote teams in isolation are also potentially more wasteful per capita than big businesses because of the level of duplication. And PLRD remote teams, particularly in the case of those who work from home, are at risk of isolating and disengaging their people, where top performers lose the collaboration they had access to in the home office.

Today, these are issues experienced by an elite few businesses. However, as the trend of entrepreneurship continues to grow and develop more and more toward these advanced businesses, the infrastructure issues must be dealt with sooner rather than later.

BRANCH OFFICES

The biggest problem most branch offices face, particularly when they cross cultural divides (such as western companies opening branch offices in Asia or vice versa), is that they are sending their teams into the unknown. They are putting their employees into an environment with a culture and experience that they can't control.

The culture of a workspace is incredibly important and it's closely related with employer branding - the way companies attract, retain and develop and grow talent. Company culture is the reason that companies like Google and Facebook manage to attract some of the world's brightest minds, without paying top tier wages in their industry; they know that the branding and experience of working for them is such that it is more important than financial remuneration alone.

The next challenge that a lot of branch offices face is technological. If a company is large enough to require branch offices, it will generally have above average IT requirements. Such companies need additional data security and they want to make sure their teams are very well-connected. It's important to avoid burdening a small team with the weight of a corporate IT system.

Branch offices are also trying to administer their teams remotely, perhaps from the U.S. or the U.K. where they have their IT team, which presents another challenge. The first issue is the eight- to fifteen-hour time difference. The branch office has to sort out printer drivers and day-to-day IT headaches while very far away from their IT team. This presents a bit of a nightmare for the support team. Beyond IT, some companies even have centralised HR and centralised payroll, which are also quite challenging to manage from afar.

FLYING SQUADS

The most common approach branch offices take when expanding to a new market is to send what I call a 'flying squad' of between three and five people from their head office to gauge interest in the new market. The team is given a mandate for a year or two to drive sales, build relationships and demonstrate that there's a big enough market in the new location to warrant a larger presence.

The challenge with this approach is that the team has a finite period of time to reach the company's goals, yet no one is exactly sure if that time period will be enough. They may need to stay longer, or they may need to exit very quickly. If things don't go well, companies want to be able to cut their losses and run.

The way coworking solves that problem is multilevel. First of all, one of the things that's incredibly reassuring to head offices is knowing that their branch office team is being put into an environment where they not only have physical space provided for them, but a more holistic workplace experience. The coworking environment provides the necessary corporate culture; it takes over the employee engagement aspect of the workplace. The space hosts the after-work drinks, the networking and in some cases the training.

This practice relieves one of the fears with a branch office: Their team has been sent away from home, their families and their support network. Not only do they have to adjust to a new corporate environment, but they have to contend with a new culture. And, they're away from all of their existing business relationships that help them conduct their business. Coworking allows their team to get into a strong network as fast as possible and it accelerates market entry.

Branch offices provide one of the most fantastic case studies where a network is so much more valuable than a physical space. As soon as team members get into a network, they are able to access qualified professionals such as web developers, lawyers and people that can help with corporate services and company setup. All of their needs are met through introductions and word-of-mouth referral once they are in that network. The knowledge base of a coworking environment is incredibly vast and valuable.

Beyond a professional standpoint, that network puts them in a position to start building friendships. Interpersonal connections are what will support people when they go through the adjustment of a relocation and what will make them far more likely to stay at their assignment.

An article written by Rob Chipman, President of FIDI and CEO of Asian Tiger Mobility, looked at the cost of sending a family overseas. While figures will vary depending on individual circumstance and role, the article revealed that the sunk cost to an organisation for moving a key person overseas is approximately $400,000. Chipman's calculation included the costs of repatriation, training and school fees, but did not include the cost of maintaining any pension schemes back home. [10]

In addition to the $400,000 sunk cost, according to estimates by INSEAD, there is between a 10 to 50 percent chance that an expatriate placement will fail and the person will repatriate within twelve months. Only 60 percent of that sunk cost delivers value to the organisation. The rest is simply lost. When a company decides to send team members overseas, they carry a risk factor of around $200,000 per person. Regardless of the size of the organisation, it is very important that the position is successful. [11]

At Collective Works, international branch offices whose team members stay with us generally have a very high success rate. Very few branch offices that enter the Singapore market through Collective Works don't stay in the market. However, we have seen some branch offices enter initially through us, then get their own offices elsewhere and subsequently fall apart.

For example, a former client of ours was a British tech company. The parent company was worth hundreds of millions of pounds. They sent over a sales team of three to Singapore with a mandate to look after Australia, New Zealand, as well as Asia Pacific. When they first moved, they were one of Collective Work's early bespoke clients. Bespoke is a service we provide to custom build space for our members. They had come from a really beautiful office, with great amenities. The team had been a little bit indulged in their home location, so they were indulged at Collective Works as well.

Collective Works customized their office to make it special for them. We imported acoustic dampening foam and lined the walls of their office with it in a zigzag formation. Then we flew in acoustic clouds, which were made of organic sheep's wool, from Somerset in the U.K. We hung the clouds from the ceiling to give the team a richly insulated acoustic environment that absorbed sound, so they wouldn't disturb each other when on the phone. The team was very successful while at Collective Works; they hit all of their sales targets.

However, after twenty-four months with us, they decided that they wanted a lot more space. They left Collective Works and rented a 2,000-square-foot heritage shophouse. Remember that they only had three staff, so that was a lot of space. Within twelve months at the new location, the team disbanded and joined other companies and the company exited the Singapore market.

I can't say that outcome was entirely due to their leaving a coworking environment at such a small size, but it certainly played a factor. Sadly, whenever we ran into any of the team members afterwards and asked how they were getting on in their new space, they'd say, 'It's great, but it's kind of lonely.' People are usually very reluctant to admit they're lonely. To bring it up in a business context means it was something that was quite acutely felt.

CASE STUDY — DROPBOX — AN EMPLOYER THAT VALUES HUMAN CAPITAL

My company, Collective Works, looks after the Asia Pacific team of a company called Dropbox. A lot of people are familiar with Dropbox; it's a large, very successful internet startup that democratized cloud computing and made it easy to share files. The Asia Pacific team of Dropbox consists of a satellite office of only four people; these team members are charming, incredibly intelligent and they spend a significant amount of time on the road.

Dropbox demonstrates a huge commitment to corporate culture; the company shows the people working for them how important their wellbeing and wellness are to the organisation.

When we signed on this Dropbox team, Dropbox actually dispatched a Cultural Ambassador to come out to Singapore from Australia. Her job was to make sure this satellite team was loved, looked after and experiencing their work lives in the Dropbox vision of how work should be.

A couple of days before the ambassador arrived, she sent me an email to help her prepare for the team's arrival. She asked for addresses of furniture companies, locations of nearby supermarkets and flower shops where she could buy plants. We then organized a Skype call to discuss how to make the environment most conducive for her team. We removed furniture and created more space. We reconfigured power points. She insisted that we install a minibar. She asked about local printers in Singapore where she could print art, wall vinyls and graphics for the team's space.

I had never before experienced a company that paid so much attention to the working environment their team was in, that they went to the extent to have a cultural custodian within their organisation. The company flew someone out specifically to ensure that their team's environment was of the culture and standard that Dropbox leaders expected for themselves. They'd come into a space that was already highly provisioned with many luxuries and put more on top; they wanted to add their own unique flavour, they wanted it to feel like home.

Within the ambassador's whirlwind visit, she managed to buy sofas, coffee tables and art and to have them all installed. She had light fittings modified, arranged little plants, fully stocked the fridge and set up a grocery subscription so the team had healthy refreshments upon arrival. She was overjoyed when she heard we had our own local coffee roaster that produced custom blend coffee and batch roasts, which was similar to Dropbox's own coffee culture in San Francisco.

Dropbox, being such a successful company with a clearly defined brand and corporate image, understood the importance of culture and community as part of their organisation. Even though their team was spread out across the world, the company culture among the offices was common. The experience was common. That infrastructure in return made a company that was stronger and more cohesive, giving these remote teams a sense of identity and a sense of belonging.

Beyond the environment, every month Dropbox sent their team members cultural handbooks, posters and little gifts and toys and t-shirts that they could give away. In effect, they gave them networking tools - gifts they could offer to help them engage with their peers and build personal relationships. The amount of thought and consideration behind these actions is quite profound; not only did these gestures create a happier workforce, but a more productive workforce.

AGILE MNCs

One significant challenge for many multinational corporations (MNCs) is real estate overhead. Another challenge is lack of flexibility and the burden of legacy. And a third challenge would be the fight for talent in an increasingly competitive marketplace and the need to battle the perception of being a little bit dated in that market.

Today, many MNCs are pushing to become decentralised; they have realised they have to stop trying to run the world from New York or London and aim to have a diffused management team achieving lean gains globally. Large corporations have realised their centralised structures leave money on the table by failing to address local market need in a fast and relevant enough way and they are now trying to tap into technology in order to change the way they do business.

Traditionally, large businesses have maintained a few choice nodes around the world; they aren't so much decentralised as they are centralised in several places. This arrangement really limits the flexibility offered to their team members. When we look at work place satisfaction surveys, companies like Google and Facebook - tech companies with creative, flexible working environments consistently rank highest.

When the younger generations are interviewed, in Singapore specifically, 70 percent of Gen Y workers surveyed said that flexible work arrangements are their number one preference in an employer. People really want to choose when, where and how they work. A nodal, nine-to-five MNC doesn't allow that flexibility. Thus, a multinational corporation's traditional working environ-ment limits their ability to attract star talent.

Multinationals are very rarely real estate companies. Usually they're financial services, technology, pharmaceutical, manufacturing, fast-moving-consumer-goods (FMCG) or commodity companies. They have nothing to do with real estate. Yet, real estate for them represents an incredibly large line item on the P&L and it's typically a line item that is immovable. It sits high on the list as a fixed cost and is considered completely inflexible. Their real estate overhead is fixed for many years in advance.

Interestingly, companies assign such a big international expense line to managing an area of their business that is not their core area of expertise. This evolved out of a traditional business mindset of wanting to control every aspect of operation. Commitment to that control, however, forces those businesses to miss the modern-day opportunities presented by a collaborative economy.

The apparent simplicity of real estate tricks people into thinking they are best qualified to make their own purchasing decisions, or that they are best qualified to manage them. Traditionally, MNCs have managed their real estate, or working environments, through a network of agents, designers and subcontractors. At every level of those transactions, someone is making a commission and nobody is incentivized to be efficient. In fact, this structure guarantees inefficiency.

Landlords traditionally love MNCs because they're stable. They take very long-term leases and they don't vary their square footage significantly. It has been the status quo for a long period of time. The challenge now is that the status quo doesn't suit the way that people want to work. But today, even MNCs are not immune to large shifts in square footage.

In order to shift to a solution, the first realisation that needs to be made is that perhaps the heads of multinational companies are not the best people to manage their own real estate - they aren't at an advantage to do so. The second shift that needs to occur is that the company must develop a sense of trust that their employees can work independently - that they can govern themselves and remain productive on their own. Finally, MNCs need to realise that only certain elements of their corporation can and should actually be decentralised. Back office processing and security functions, for example, arc all appalling areas for decentralisation.

Clearly, there's a very strong cost rationale about why MNCs should look at these factors (namely current office utilisation rates), but there's a competitive advantage and quality of life rationale to consider as well. More and more people are thinking of ways that older-age adults and young people can work flexibly. We're looking at a generation of people now that may never retire or may retire very late in their lives. People care more about the quality of their working lives on an ongoing basis, because they're realizing that they won't get to stop working. They recognize the need to make the journey more enjoyable, instead of working for retirement, or working for the destination.

The risk for multinational companies is that when they're that large, it's very easy to hide inefficiency; it's very easy for people to show up and collect a salary and not do an awful lot. If a company or individual wants something done and done extremely well, they go to an industry specialist - somebody who is incentivised to work in that area. People in coworking are incentivised to make real estate incredibly efficient; they work in an environment where relationships are flexible, not fixed. In a coworking environment, there is a real possibility that the operator could lose their clients if the clients aren't satisfied. If the space isn't functional or if people feel that they aren't getting great value for their money out of the space, they will leave.

The whole coworking model - the flexibility that it offers - creates a huge accountability loop. Clients continually choose to re-contract on a month-by-month basis because they are pleased with the service that they're getting. That decision to re-contract keeps the whole system honest; it is like dating long-term as opposed to being married. Interestingly, nothing like that has ever existed in corporate real estate before. Nothing like that has ever existed in a MNC structure. The beauty of this arrangement is that MNCs don't have to restructure; they don't have to adopt this model and take on this risk. What they can do is simply leverage it.

With the increasing sophistication of coworking environments, the space can host if not outright handle all of the complex IT requirements that MNCs need. Many coworking environments will allow companies to install their own IT backend and their own firewalls. At Collective Works, we have client server rooms and we can even run private wifi within our space if we need to, in order to support decentralised MNC clients. The price per head that the MNC will be charged back is real and accountable and since it's not paying a fixed price for space - whether its utilised or not - it represents a massive cost saving.

BUSINESS CONTINUITY PLANNING

One of the planning challenges faced by organisations is the challenge of point risk. What if their headquarters is affected by a natural disaster or is, in some ways, incapacitated? The cost to a company of losing a key location is massive. It's inconceivable to most of us, but fundamentally shutting down the headquarters of a large organisation, for even a period of days, can result in a cost of millions, if not hundreds of millions in lost revenue and recovery costs.

In an increasingly fast-paced and connected world, the issue of business continuity planning is one that's incredibly important. The interesting opportunity for businesses is that by leveraging coworking environments in the markets where they operate, they're able to not only provide a business continuity solution, but also reduce point risk. They have a live, second office away from their headquarters, which is already connected to their network and connected to their global infrastructure. Business resilience is improved and recovery time from an incident is vastly reduced by using the coworking network.

With this model, companies create a better working environment. They have no drop in connectivity or efficiency, but potentially create a far more engaging and dynamic environment, which is more likely to encourage staff retention and growth. The model also eliminates the ivory tower syndrome that so many MNCs suffer from, where its employees sit around in their own beautiful buildings, thinking the same ideas. In the coworking model, their team members are exposed to people from outside their corporate bubble. They can learn what people really think about their company and about problems in the market that they could potentially solve.

CHAPTER SIX TAKEAWAYS

▶ Coworking is a method that can be applied in a number of different ways to different markets with different needs. The origins of coworking may have begun with small businesses, but very quickly multinational or large corporate real estate consumers have realised that the benefits of the coworking methodology can also be applied to their businesses.

▶ While they need the same facilities as big businesses, PLRD businesses can lack the purchasing power to access them. And PLRD businesses, particularly in the case of solopreneurs who work from home, can be very isolating, where top performers lose the collaboration they had access to in the corporate world. Coworking is therefore a viable solution.

▶ Coworking presents an opportunity for branch office members to more easily enter into a new culture. Not only do they have physical space provided for them, but the after-work drinks, the networking and the training. This helps companies attract, retain and develop and grow talent.

▶ For MNCs to position themselves to attract the best talent, they need to move toward a flexible arrangement for their team members and foster an attitude of employee trust. A flexible arrangement also reduces costs.

▶ Traditionally, MNCs have managed their real estate through a network of agents, designers and subcontractors. That structure lends itself to inefficiency. Coworking environments, on the other hand, are incentivised to be efficient.

▶ By leveraging a coworking environment, companies are able to not only provide a business continuity solution, but also to reduce point risk. With a live, second office away from their headquarters that is already connected to their network and connected to their global infrastructure, business resilience is vastly improved.

THE VALUE PROPOSITION TO MEMBERS

A colleague I've known for a number of years came to my office, grappling with a business dilemma. Stephen is a British-born expat living in Singapore, working as a Senior Executive in a large financial institution. He manages millions of square feet of real estate for a company with 7,000 employees in Singapore and over 80,000 employees globally - a real estate portfolio with an annual run-rate in excess of a billion dollars each year.

Stephen has a stressful job. It's his role to juggle the constant mismatch between need and supply in his business. He must battle the company's rapidly fluctuating need for space, forcing him to have to make decisions quickly and without all the information he needs. It's a situation which inevitably means many of the real estate commitments he makes will end up being incompatible with the needs of the business - the company constantly has too much or too little space at any point in time.

The day he came to my office, Stephen shared that he needed to find space for 2,500 additional people in the next two years – a 36 percent increase in size. The space he was seeking would have to be around 300,000 square feet in traditionally planned space. In Singapore, where office vacancy was around 4 percent at the time, finding a building with that much space available in his time frame and within his company's budget was proving problematic.

Stephen's problem wasn't just about finding enough space for desks. He needed to supply the company with additional room for a safe operating margin and room for amenities: meeting spaces, breakout spaces, canteens and maybe even a napping room - all the modern demands employees are now placing on companies. At the same time, he was being asked to cut costs. How could he juggle these diametrically opposed problems?

Professionally, he is constantly stuck between a rock and a hard place. He is paid to own this problem and the decision makers above him are so far removed from the situation on the ground that they don't really consider the scale of the challenge, let alone the financial implications of what they're asking for.

Stephen wanted to find a flexible and scalable solution that would smooth out all the peaks and troughs, so he could consistently perform and match his real estate to his headcount. And, he really wanted to outsource the problem. Let's look at how coworking could help.

DON'T PAY FOR VACANCY

When Stephen came to me with the need to find desks for 2,500 people, I began to think about the engineering and mechanisms required to allow coworking to cater to that scale of client. There are a couple of conflicting challenges when dealing with large clients and managing a coworking community for a need that large. As a general rule, I don't allow more than 20 to 30 percent of a space to be occupied by one company; doing so changes the global personality of the coworking environment, potentially to the detriment of other members.

Therefore, to support a 2,500-desk requirement, a coworking operator would need a membership base of either 8,500, or it would need to create a 'safe space' for the company so that their membership would be seen as a benefit. In other words, the operator would create a private environment that is safe and secure for the client, but also safe for the coworking community. Placing the company's team in a private space would protect the community from being dominated by such a strong culture; their presence would be a benefit to the coworking community at large if placed within a space that benefited from access to a big bank.

Because of the nature of coworking, Stephen could spread out his 2,500 people into coworking environments all across Singapore and subscribe to corporate plans across a number of operators. But here's the catch - Stephen was saying he will need 2,500 desks, but he doesn't yet know when and at what pace they will be needed. Even larger organisations don't just add on

2,500 people in a short time period; it happens gradually and the total capacity is a best-guess estimate that could be over or under.

Stephen's headcount is variable and it will change year to year. The company may never hit that 2,500 mark, or they could exceed it. The first benefit for using a coworking environment is that, structured correctly, the company won't have to pay for vacancy or at the very least they wouldn't have to pay for as much of it. This benefit is because the company's relationship is tied to headcount instead of just square footage alone.

In coworking, memberships or subscriptions are structured more like a gym or a club. Think of the space as a clubhouse. A membership grants the member a certain quantum of access; the coworking operator has a spectrum on memberships based on the use cases they come across. Because such licenses and memberships are not captured under leasing law, it allows coworking environments to be a lot more flexible with their members when compared with a traditional lease.

In the absence of a subscription and a partner to provide the service, Stephen's only option would be to rent and furnish approximately 300,000 square feet and hold it in advance of his user requirement. Again, even the best designed corporate offices will only achieve between 60 and 70 percent desk utilisation at any given time, but in this high-growth scenario the over commitment of space for two years is significantly more wasteful than low utilisation in stabilized operations.

RAPID START AND STOP - THE ON/OFF BUTTON

The second benefit to coworking for someone in Stephen's position is that coworking is turnkey. As soon as he hires somebody, the coworking operator can get the new team member plugged in and up and running within twenty-four hours, if not less. This rapid-start model also holds great appeal because it outsources the entire process. With coworking, if the company already has a subscription, they can just add an extra person onto it. Done.

At Collective Works, one of our memberships offers a rolling thirty-day option. At any point in time, you can write to us and say, 'I would like to stop my membership in thirty days.' The ability to 'turn off' rental space is profoundly radical in real estate. Traditionally, the real estate industry favours long-term, locked-in revenue resulting in people often being contractually bound longer than they would like to be. If a company were to take a five- or ten-year lease and in three years' time, the space is too big or too small for them, they're still stuck.

Real estate uses these traditional long-term contractual requirements to force tenants to find replacement tenants to take over their commitments or pay a penalty (in some cases the balance of the agreement) or forfeit their deposit. All of these measures are designed to reduce the cost of tenant acquisition, reduce churn and make more money for the asset owner. There are a lot of engineering and regulatory strings in leases. With the advent of a much more client-driven approach of coworking, the structure of inconveniencing the tenant for the benefit of the property owner is fast approaching its expiration date.

What business decision makers want is the ability to change their minds. To a small business, that ability de-risks the decision, to a large business it represents P&L engineering and an ability to become more agile. Leasing is always a laboured and negotiated decision: Business operators are forced to balance term with operating cost and asset owners incur significant marketing and transaction costs. Interestingly, the need is the same regardless of business size because in today's dynamic world, the centuries-old leasing structure isn't keeping pace.

CAPITAL LIGHT AND DE-RISKED

Capital expenditure are the funds used by a company to set up a physical business – also termed as spend to balance sheet. CapEx is a term more often used by industrial companies where the sums are hundreds of millions or billions of dollars, but every business effectively has CapEx and OpEx, or operating costs. For most businesses, CapEx is a lot more stressful, because it's money that is spent upfront before there is any money coming in, whereas OpEx is money that is spent while there is a running cash flow, so the business is in more of a steady state.

One of the great value propositions of coworking is it offsets upfront capital expenditure and thus greatly reduces the startup capital needed to get a business off the ground for a client. All the CapEx costs get amortised into just the subscription fee and are normalized as operating expenses.

While that model does produce a higher per square foot OpEx, it may take two or three years for these normalized operating expenses to start to equal the equivalent spend the company would have encountered to setup a private office. Therefore, the increase is not so significant to be challenging. But, all this is before the added value of the free cashflow over that period is taken into account.

Without this cashflow smoothing effect of the subscription, many businesses and branch offices would require significantly more capital to get off the ground. Add to that factor the added business benefit of being part of a business community designed to help the business meet its goals and it's clearly a winning scenario.

Looking at corporates, the potential to assist with capital spend is even more dramatic. Take, for example, the bank which shuttered five floors of its office tower because it subscribed for 80,000 additional square feet than it needed. That process in real terms represents a multi-million-dollar write-down of undepreciated fitout and a horrific ecological footprint. The entire process would have been eliminated had the bank been leveraging a coworking environment to provide its flex space. The space would have been repurposed by the operator for another client; the space would have continued in use and the bank would have saved millions in operating expenses for vacant space and the balance sheet write down.

Coworking presents large companies with an opportunity to outsource a percentage of their CapEx and reduce their vacancy risk.

FIT-RIP-REPEAT

There are times when I look at the normal way of doing things and think, there has to be a better way. In the traditional approach to commercial real estate, units are leased to tenants bare. Tenants fit them out and at the end of their tenancy agreement, they're required to reinstate the units back to bare, or in other words remove all the customization, fit-out furniture, decoration and services that they installed to make the unit serviceable. They make the space a blank slate again for the next tenant.

I can understand where this process came from. This arrangement was fine years ago when businesses stayed in the same spot for twenty years. But, in today's business environment where the pace of business is so much faster, this process leaves an unfortunate ecological footprint. I call this process fit out, rip out, repeat. The process is enormously time consuming, costly and ecologically wasteful. And even when we factor in the recycling of gypsum (as it can be 100 percent recycled down to new gypsum board) and in some cases, even the electrical cabling, what's happening in this process is that a completely serviceable fit is being thrown away. Energy is being wasted to recycle and reuse and repurpose these materials. And then the unit is being fitted in a similar fashion again by the next tenant.

Businesses and landlords plan for this process. It's the status quo and that means often spaces aren't fitted as well as they could be. If you know the renovation work you'll be undertaking will be thrown away, you design the space to be thrown away.

There is a better way. Coworking provides a medium to reduce physical waste, to break this fit out, rip out, repeat cycle and to build environments that are better and more conducive to the people working in them.

It's not uncommon, even in a fast-paced city like Singapore, for a business centre to go without major renovation for ten to fifteen years. So, when a space is fitted well, it's fitted with good quality materials, good quality planning and it's continuously iterated and revised and fine- tuned to continue to suit its market. We completely avoid the fit out, rip out, repeat cycle.

And as well as being ecological, avoiding that cycle has a really significant cash advantage to businesses. Avoiding significant initial cutbacks in renovation and amortising or spreading that cost over a running office for as long as a company needs, is hugely beneficial. It also presents us with an opportunity to build better environments for our people because it's worth investing in space that will persist. Better designed, healthier environments are another significant benefit to occupants of coworking spaces.

ACCESS TO THE KNOWLEDGE BASE

Coworking provides an ability to not only get started very quickly, but to get started very deeply. As opposed to the traditional approach of starting a new business or hiring a new employee - which I liken to getting into the shallow end of the pool then slowly working one's way in - starting a business in a coworking environment is a swan dive into the deep end. The business team is immediately immersed in its new surroundings and deeply involved in a new community.

The relationship-building aspects of market entry as well as physical infrastructure are quite exhilarating. To be successful, a business needs not only the equipment and facilities, it also needs the people and the relationships. The latter is something that's missing from any other market entry product.

The value of an increased network is an increased likelihood of success. The direct commercial outcome of an increased network and reach would be increased sales, but there's also an increased supply of wellbeing. When people feel more connected, with a greater sense of belonging in the environment in which they work, they are happier and will stay in those environments longer.

Leveraging the knowledge base requires tapping into an inherited or host network to find the relevant knowledge and previous experience that can help a business or provide that business with a different perspective on the way that it operates. Coworking members share ideas and experiences with each other in a trusted environment. This model demonstrates a return to the traditional values of relationship-based business. It isn't the way business has been done for a while, but it is incredibly powerful when properly leveraged.

In a shared facility, leveraging the network is first about the available knowledge and experience, but second about profile and partnership. By being part of a network, a business operator has the ability first to make other members and their respective companies aware that their company exists and second to partner with them and achieve more than what could normally be achieved. That network can be used to promote the business and expand its offering and company skillset without expanding its overheads.

Access to a network solves another critical challenge that companies often face - lack of opportunities to socialise. By socialisation, I don't mean beer and chit-chat. I mean the socialisation of ideas and concepts – although a beer after work never hurts either. In a recent meeting with the head of asset management at a global corporate, this lack of socialization was amusingly termed as the 'inbreeding of ideas' which I think is a really great way of explaining the concept to both small and large businesses. Consideration has to be taken to avoid this: When you're talking to the same people all the time and your ideas and perspectives align, the gene pool is reduced and ideas aren't stress-tested. Everybody has been drinking the same Kool-Aid.

By giving business leaders access to the knowledge and experience of these new networks, by providing them with different perspectives or improving their businesses, their leadership can be transformed. Many business leaders feel isolated and believe they need to do everything themselves, often reinventing the wheel in the process. Access to a network of other business leaders who may have experienced the same challenges offers opportunities for mentorship and idea sharing. This practice forms the basis of the concept behind EO, the

Entrepreneurs Organisation, but through colocation it suddenly becomes real time and far more powerful.

In a shared facility where PLRD business leaders have access to a network of other businesses, leveraging that network is also about synergistically building each other's businesses and profiles by forming strategic partnerships. By being part of a network, PLRD business leaders have the opportunity to make more established businesses aware that they exist and to achieve more by partnering with them than they'd be able to achieve on their own.

Ideas need diversity and fresh stimulus to grow, so having a really narrow world perspective or a perspective limited by a single corporate culture is a universal problem for small or big businesses. Businesses need to be exposed to external opinions or external stimuli.

A BETTER WORKING LIFE EXPERIENCE

Generation Y may never retire. Western pension schemes can't afford them to. And more importantly, Generation Y doesn't want to delay living until retirement, unlike their parents. They want to live while they work.

These expectations create a very different set of demands on an employer. Today the offices of the world's most aspirational companies provide free meals, basketball courts and fitness centres, games rooms, relaxation and meditation spaces, yoga and, most importantly, they are seriously Instagrammable. Employers are looked upon to help people live their best lives, not just provide a source of income anymore.

All of these demands create a challenge. Suddenly, in the fight for talent, paying one's team well and providing them with health insurance isn't enough. Doing what used to make a company a model employer now makes them part of the sea of average companies that people don't want to work for. And the cost of changing the status quo is considerable. The great news is that the right coworking space, one that is a culturally matched space for a business, can provide the amenities, lifestyle, engagement and the autonomy and flexible working arrangements that this generation requires.

What if a business's office wasn't a fixed cost? What if their physical environment actually helped attract, retain and motivate its people? What if a company's physical space actually made their employees more productive and more satisfied? Now that's food for thought.

FRACTIONAL LUXURY

For the average consumer, fractional luxury demonstrates the concept of leverage in action. Fractional luxury is a term I use to describe a situation where someone can rent something they might not have been able to buy outright. The concept isn't new. It is the ability to book a five-star hotel room, rather than buy a property for your holiday. More recently, it is the ability to rent a designer handbag for $150 a month, rather than spending $5,500 to buy it outright (a service provided by the multi-million-dollar business Bag, Borrow or Steal).

Timeshares, hire-purchase agreements, car leases, country club memberships and exotic car clubs are all examples of fractional luxury.

My personal favourite example of fractional luxury is the tech startup, Uber. Uber created an app that enables limousine drivers to be booked directly by customers, on demand and by proximity. Before I moved to Singapore I drove a black, three-litre Mercedes with a cream leather interior. I loved that car. When I moved to Singapore, I naively thought I would buy another one. However, after a short call to Mercedes-Benz Singapore I learned that the purchase price of the $51,000 car I had just left behind was approximately $277,000 due to duties and levies in Singapore.

Singapore is one of the most expensive countries in the world in which to buy and own a car. There are many government disincentives when it comes to car ownership to prevent the city-state from becoming gridlocked. Whether I could afford to purchase the car or not, my business brain would never rationalize the purchase, financing, or depreciation of a $277,000 car that should have cost less than a quarter of that price. Because of companies like Uber, I will never have to; I can pay to have a Mercedes and a driver take me to work every day and it will take me about twelve years of Uber fares to hit the purchase price of that car.

Beyond the ability to leverage a small investment to access toys and resources one may not have had the ability to purchase outright, fractional luxury has a second benefit: the reduction of waste. It is a form of shared economy. For example, if you purchase a home for your annual four-week holiday, you have invested in a property (or a mortgage for a property) that may be empty for eleven months of the year. By buying a timeshare, booking a hotel room or leasing an apartment, not only do you benefit from a lower cost of entry, but the property can also be used by other holiday-goers at other times of the year. And, you may even enjoy additional services and amenities that you wouldn't have enjoyed otherwise.

By taking the focus away from owning, not only are you able to achieve more, you are able to achieve a higher level of quality and service on an individual basis while paying less because you are only purchasing the quantum you need. In that regard, you can access skills and equipment without paying for the whole facility. Why buy the taxi just to get you to where you are going? Ultimately, fractional luxury eliminates waste without reducing experience or enjoyment.

A perfect example of someone who has learned how to take advantage of fractional luxury was one of Collective Works' knowledge workers, a guy called Marco. Marco is Italian, very elegant, a chic guy with an evergreen tan. He ran a marketing consultancy with just himself and a laptop. Marco would spend his summer in Europe traveling through Ibiza and London and Paris, renting expensive villas, visiting very famous nightclubs, traveling business class and having the most wonderful life. Then he'd fly back to Asia in October, take up a coworking membership for the winter and work before returning to Europe to party when the weather improved.

He had it down. He made a lot of money and he spent a lot of money. The space in Singapore was essentially turnkey for him. Everything was set up and ready for him when he needed it. He had his meetings with clients, took care of business and then checked out and went to live the wonderful life of an international playboy.

While it's not the kind of lifestyle everybody would want, he had taken control of the kind of lifestyle he wanted and found a way to structure it. He leveraged his resources and network and IT when he needed it and then turned it all off - he only paid for what he was using. By being incredibly efficient, he was gaining access to a quality of life that he wouldn't have been able to afford otherwise.

COWORKING AND LEVERAGE

Coworking represents the ability to leverage physical facilities, knowledge and a larger network. Coworking spaces have their own physical facilities and infrastructure and all they ask of their clients is a monthly subscription payment to access the network and all the equipment and potential contained within. Coworking presents companies with the possibility of living and working anywhere without having to create their own infrastructure.

The reality of real estate is that modern office buildings and industrial facilities have been designed with large occupant teams in mind. From an engineering perspective, this makes sense; having a large floor plate that centralises heating, cooling, circulation and utilities increases floor plate efficiency. However, this model is a reflection of the types of businesses that existed when this genre of construction became the norm.

Businesses have evolved and their needs have changed. With the increase of profitable and powerful PLRD businesses there has been a drive to decrease centralised footprints of multinational teams and a real-estate mismatch has been created. The problem is that it is quite challenging to separate large floorplate commercial buildings into individual units that are the right size for small international teams; to do so is incredibly wasteful and complex.

To chop up a 40,000-square-foot floor plate into sixty-six, private 600-square-foot offices one would need to create an internal labyrinth of corridors, each office would need its own electrical distribution board and meter and most of those sixty-six offices would never see windows. Floorplates of that size would typically be designed to subdivide into no more than perhaps six to eight parts. However, by keeping the space combined and adding a service layer of coworking, it suddenly becomes possible to turn that same floorplate into a shared but managed facility for sixty-six companies or more.

Modifying these large spaces for PLRD users reinvigorates the world's existing real estate stock, allows the best of both worlds environmentally and functionally and gives new potential to buildings that aren't currently right-sized for today's agile business environment.

While the cloud has done a lot to bridge the capability gap between large and PLRD businesses, without the coworking model, a PLRD business's ability to acquire and even access top-end equipment in every environment they work in is reduced; cutting-edge equipment is generally quite expensive. In the coworking model, the coworking environment could buy top-of-the-range equipment that functions better and has features that its cheaper counterparts would not have. By renting coworking environments, PLRD businesses have access to high-end equipment without having to purchase it themselves.

Other examples of amenities include meeting room facilities, prime locations, an IT network, internet connection and higher-end technology, many of which aren't otherwise available to PLRD businesses. This new perspective on economy of scale also allows us to transform inefficient, large and wasteful ways of working into a more eco-friendly and sustainable model.

Coworking allows these PLRD businesses to act like accordion businesses: To meet the demands of their changing client landscape, the businesses inhale a volume of new temporary staff or form business partnerships. A two-person outfit expands to six, eight or ten people in size. They achieve great things and at the end of the project they exhale and shrink back to two. It's the professional end of the gig economy where people deliver remarkable value and flow to where they are needed. And the best part is that the talent can be sourced from within the community.

By contrast, imagine the typical business owner that wants to increase the skillset within their business. In a traditional business environment, they would need to hire new employees, which entails a range of recruitment and training costs before that employee can start becoming profitable. Moreover, if the new employee is not fully utilised (unlike a contractor or visiting specialist) there is no way to moderate their payment or overheads to the business. This model contains all the associated costs of scaling the business with none of the lean gains and eventually will also necessitate additional costs of expanding offices, taking on larger facilities and expanding into them.

Business leaders need to find a balance between the inconvenience and disruption of moving and having an office that is right-sized, without being so large that it would be wasteful nor so small that it would impact productivity. In most cases, the outcome is that the business will oversubscribe and often pay for more room than it actually needs. I call this "the Growth Inefficiency Paradigm,' meaning businesses desire to grow, but this optimism for growth requires headroom and that headroom expands their cost base and worsens their efficiency and profitability at a time when they are already stretching.

It has long been accepted that to grow, businesses have to make these sacrifices and undertake 'J-Curve' investments (investments that lose money in the short term but will eventually pay dividends). The question to ask was why grow in the first place? Often it had something to do with sustainability and longevity and in other cases it was about meeting greater demands and making greater profits.

But what if there was a different way to create sustainability and longevity and make greater profits without exploding a company's cost base? In a coworking environment, a business can outsource tasks to a different business using the same space, that specializes in the area that they were looking for. Because the two businesses are proximate, the business leaders can work closely with each other and experience the benefits of having hired an employee without the headaches that come along with a new hire. Then the PLRD business owner can choose to work with this new company as much or as little as they like.

That is a reality of coworking. Instead of taking on the entire cost base for the physical environment and additional human talent by itself, a business can share the cost with a larger business community. If a company chooses to scale, its environment will allow it to do so without paying for the extra space before it needs it. Today, larger coworking environments can manage the scaling of teams to over 100 people in size. Teams can simply expand within the space resulting in minimal downtime, with no change of address and no waste.

Now try and do that in your normal office setup.

CHAPTER SEVEN TAKEAWAYS

▶ The headcount of large companies is variable and it will change year to year. The benefit of using a coworking environment is that a company doesn't have to pay for vacancy, it only pays per head.

▶ Coworking is turnkey; as soon as a company hires somebody, the coworking environment can get the new team member plugged in and up and running within twenty-four hours, if not less. Likewise, if an employee leaves, companies can easily cancel the membership and not have to pay additional overhead costs.

▶ Coworking provides the ability for new employees not only to get started very quickly, but to get started very deeply. They are immediately immersed in their new surroundings and involved in a new community.

▶ The direct commercial outcome of increased network and reach would be increased sales, but also there's an increased supply of wellbeing. When people feel more connected, they are happier and will stay in those environments longer.

▶ By being part of a network, businesses have the ability first to make other members and their respective companies aware that they exist and second to partner with them and achieve more than they normally would be able to achieve.

▶ The right coworking space can provide the amenities, lifestyle, engagement and most importantly, the autonomy and flexible working arrangements that this generation requires.

▶ With fractional luxury, someone can pay a small amount to rent something they might not have been able to buy outright. In the coworking model, the coworking environment grants businesses access to resources and networks they perhaps couldn't afford or create alone.

▶ In a coworking environment, a business can outsource tasks to a different business using the same space that specializes in the area of need. Because the two businesses are proximate, the business leaders can work closely with each other and experience the benefits of having hired an employee without the headaches and overheads that come along with a new hire.

Chapter Eight

VALUE PROPOSITIONS TO BUILDING OWNERS

REDUCE COSTS OF ACQUISITION AND ACCESS UNIQUE SALES CHANNELS

The sales cycle in coworking is entirely unlike the traditional real estate sales cycle. The transaction doesn't involve a broker - it's directly conducted between the client and the space - and the clients themselves undertake the research and arrange their viewings. The coworking spaces prequalify and select the clients they want.

With coworking spaces, clients are far more interested in environmental cues than a usual real estate transaction - simply looking for the right number of desks, the right number of chairs, or a certain quantum square footage isn't enough. In my belief, circumventing the traditional real estate channels is a sign that the coworking buyer doesn't expect or consider current real estate sales channels as sufficient or sophisticated enough to meet their needs.

After years of working with entrepreneurs and business leaders, I now realise that when obstacles become too great, this temperament of person researches and finds their own solution. What that means to a building owner is that a coworking space is an entirely new sales channel. It attracts a completely different temperament of tenant and one that is highly desirable and difficult to reach.

In short, a coworking space is a sales channel to disruptors. It's a sales channel to reach the business leaders that build future high-growth companies, which is exactly the temperament that businesses and buildings need to attract to continue to fill their buildings in the future.

BRANDING, POSITIONING AND STICKINESS

Branding, positioning and stickiness aren't normally attributes that are discussed often in an asset class when people talk about buildings, but in today's world we need to talk about them a bit more. When we're dealing with clients that are interested in engaging on a personal, or perhaps an emotional level, with the environment that they're working with, then branding, positioning and stickiness become very important.

In a practical context, a branded building can also affect yield. Branded buildings, or buildings that stand for something, are what are considered landmarks. They attract tenants that want to be associated with their building; they're lightning rods, they're Eiffel Towers, they're beacons of aspiration.

But let's deconstruct what actually makes a building branded. In consumer products, we talk about brand equity as being defined as the differential impact of a brand versus the rest of the market. The equity is the product's impact in terms of its visual difference, the semantic difference and usually, an improved quality of experience to the consumer. So, how are these qualities converted into a building? How is a building made to look, feel and deliver more value? And if achieved, what would that shift do to building yields?

The envelope of a building, or a building's shell, is very difficult to change once it has been constructed. But what really defines a building and creates a sense of place is the people. As I've talked about earlier in this book, people are attracted to communities. They're attracted to groups and places that share common values. With this view, it suddenly becomes quite apparent how a coworking space could contribute something to the brand and the place-making of the building.

I hasten to add that just any old coworking space won't work. It's important to understand the sense of place, the positioning and the legacy of the building and to make sure that a coworking space is used in that context. The space must align tightly with the existing temperament of the core tenants of the building and add remarkable value and differentiation to those tenants and to the like companies that would want to occupy that building. The only exception to this is when a coworking space is used as part of a deliberate redirection or gentrification strategy; in those instances, a space will be put into a location where it deliberately jars with its surroundings.

The example I can give of a very well-branded building that aligns with a very well-branded coworking space is an asset-owner-initiated project called Level 39 at Canary Wharf in London. One Canada Square, called Canary Wharf Tower, was completed in 1991 and was the first high-rise structure built as part of the Canary Wharf development. Today, Canary Wharf is very much the financial heart of London. One Canada Square itself is home to such names as Accenture, the Bank of New York Mellon, MetLife and even the National Bank of Abu Dhabi.

In 2013, the Canary Wharf group decided to found Level 39, a coworking space designed for the fintech community, which has since grown to occupy 80,000 square feet across three floors of One Canada Square. The complementary position of a prestigious fintech coworking space with one of London's most famous buildings is undeniable. And twenty-eight years on from the building's completion, One Canada Square remains highly occupied, if not 100 percent occupied on a continual basis.

While it may be difficult to attribute the success of One Canada Square to Level 39 alone, it's interesting that the asset manager behind the building saw the importance of creating a rebellion at the fringe - in creating a space for ideation and collaboration and perhaps even flexible expansion for tenants within the building. As an asset manager will tell you, a 100 percent occupied building is a blessing and a curse.

A full space is a blessing because the building is fully utilising its yield and revenue generating potential. However, from a management perspective, it is quite challenging because, should any of those tenants within the building decide to expand, there's very little or perhaps no space to accommodate them. By adding a plastic layer to a building that also has strong synergistic value and topical alignment with the ecosystem of the building, Level 39 acts as expansion space as well as a source of inspiration to the building.

Stickiness is the outcome of a well-branded building with the right positioning, the right tenant mix and the right mix of amenities within the building. Stickiness is essentially a measure of how difficult it is for someone to leave the building or how difficult it is for someone to relocate; it is a measurement of interconnection. The more relationships a client has with their environment, the stickier it is.

In real estate, the least sticky arrangement a client can have is a straight fixed-term lease. There's little value add and little connection to sense of place or the building itself. In fact, typically the only sticky factor in a straight lease arrangement is the capital cost of the fit out and how far along it is in terms of depreciation.

Amenities in facilities like Level 39 completely transform the intangible stickiness factor of a building. Yes, as a tenant of One Canada Square, a business team could move. It could find an office in a different building in a different part of London, but it will not find another office in that city with that community, with that level of prestige and that interconnectedness.

To the tenants of One Canada Square, Level 39 is outsourced research and development. It is a finger on the pulse of the emerging financial markets in London and it's the provider of an unmeasurable cool factor.

BUILDING AMENITY TO CORE TENANTS

While I hate referring to coworking as an amenity, to many corporate tenants, coworking is seen that way. It's a check in the box, very much like a building having a gym, or a swimming pool, or season parking. If we take a ruthless business-minded approach, having a coworking space in a building, to an asset owner, is a differentiating factor. It's extra points in that owner's corner when a core tenant is considering their building versus another.

INBUILT PIPELINE OF TENANTS

As discussed earlier, coworking spaces attract very different clientele than traditional leasing tenants - typically, branch offices or smaller-sized teams with high-growth profile. While this tenant profile adds dynamism and interest and excitement to a building, it also means that a coworking space is a growing pipeline. It serves as an incubator for future core tenants, which is a very attractive prospect for a building owner. Being able to grow the owner's own future core tenants, have them acclimatise, bond with and develop a relationship with the communities in and around the building is highly valuable.

Once bonded, people don't like change. The alumni of coworking spaces tend to stay within the immediate area or precinct of the centres where they got started. If a building or development is not fully occupied, the asset owner would be wise to try and set up a referral arrangement to capture and support the alumni of the coworking space within their building.

Client retention is one of the most important metrics in business. It is absolutely one of the most important metrics in leasing and if one is trying to create a branded, well-positioned sticky building or precinct, holding onto the companies that originated within the building is critically important, not to mention a way to circumvent agent's fees.

GENTRIFIED YIELDS

Coworking spaces generally operate using a model of lease arbitrage, which essentially means they densify value and generate income from a space that is a multiple of rent. But that's just the coworking space itself. The true value of a coworking space goes far beyond the financial returns the space itself directly yields.

By reducing the cost of acquisition, branding and positioning a building, acting as an amenity to core tenants, being that plastic space that never existed and increasing foot traffic and the number of desirable tenant profiles within a building, there's a much greater impact to the asset at large than just a few high-yielding floors within a building. Having a coworking space within a building presents an opportunity to the asset owner to increase yields as well as new revenue streams and that's before talking about any kind of joint venture structuring or profit sharing with the centre itself.

LONG-TERM TENANT SUBDIVISION WITHOUT SUBDIVIDING

Modern, large-floor-plate buildings do not subdivide well. Often, floors can only be split into halves or quarters and typically, the process of subdivision creates ugly common corridor space and greatly reduces the perceived prestige of a building. Tenants don't like them anymore either; long common corridors create way-finding challenges and significant parts of the building that lack natural light. A coworking layer within a building provides a building with a long-term tenant that also subdivides as a way of doing business.

The subdivision that happens within a coworking space allows a building to accommodate for significantly smaller tenants than they otherwise would be able to. Companies of perhaps two to ten headcount who may not be core tenants today, could realistically be core tenants eighteen months ahead. A coworking layer in a building provides yet another opportunity for asset owners to outsource the messy business of subdivision into an elegant and sophisticated solution, which adds value to a building instead of detracting from it.

INCREASED FOOT TRAFFIC ON GROUND FLOORS

To buildings with commercial space on the first floor or ground-level, coworking adds yet another dynamic of value. Coworking spaces are typically highly utilized; they're multi-occupied because they have hot desking and occasional members. They also have higher visitor traffic than a normal tenant. It is not uncommon for coworking spaces to significantly increase ground floor traffic in a building.

The exact quantum is a function of the size of a coworking space relative to the size of the building. Regardless, having a coworking space within the building presents an opportunity to increase foot fall for ground-floor tenants. Cafés, bars, restaurants and gyms can all benefit from high foot traffic. To the asset owner, that factor can offer a rationale that can be used to increase ground floor rent.

CHAPTER EIGHT TAKEAWAYS:

▶ A coworking space acts as a sales channel to reach the business leaders that build future high-growth companies, which is exactly the temperament that businesses and buildings need to attract to continue to fill their buildings in the future.

▶ Branding, positioning and stickiness are very important in current times. To create a branded building, the space must align tightly with the existing temperament of the core tenants of the building and add remarkable value and differentiation to those tenants and to the like companies that would want to occupy that building.

▶ Stickiness is the outcome of a well-branded building with the right positioning, the right tenant mix and the right mix of amenities within the building. It is a measure of interconnection. The more relationships a client has with their environment, the stickier it is.

▶ A coworking space serves as an incubator for future core tenants. For owners to be able to grow their own future core tenants and to have them acclimatise, bond with and develop a relationship with the communities in and around the building is highly valuable and leads to retention.

▶ A coworking layer in a building provides an opportunity for asset owners to outsource the messy business of subdivision into an elegant and sophisticated solution, which adds value to a building instead of detracting from it.

▶ To the asset owner, the high foot traffic a coworking space generates can offer a rationale that can be used to increase ground floor rent.

HOW TO TEST DRIVE A COWORKING ENVIRONMENT

There are plenty of things to look for when searching for an ideal coworking environment. If you are interested in becoming a member yourself or are searching for space on behalf of a company, this chapter outlines key factors to consider.

Before you even arrive at a venue, start your search by shortlisting spaces by location, proximity to key features such as transport and synergistic businesses. Even within that shortlist, you'll need to learn how to choose and rank coworking spaces. You can start by taking a tour of the shortlisted spaces. Bear in mind, you're not going to get everything you need on a quick thirty- or forty-minute tour. You should approach your first tour as more of a top level assessment of sociological fit.

The tour will offer an initial familiarization with the space: what the space is about, who's there and what the general energy is like. Ask yourself, 'Does this seem like the kind of environment that suits me? Does it suit the company that I'm looking for space on behalf of?' With your first viewing, that's all you're going to determine, because your senses are going to be overloaded with the sounds and smells and look of the environment.

You're going to need not only a second view, but an actual trial. Coworking environments will call it different names, but I call it a test drive. When you're approaching a coworking environment, you're making an investment purchase. You're looking at a long-term relationship, because that's how you're going to get the most out of the space.

What we're going to outline in this chapter is what you should look for - what you should have your eyes, ears and nose open to while doing a tour. Some of these criteria you'll pick up on during a quick scan of the space and others you'll need to consider via deeper analysis. The more information you have going into a tour, the more you're going to get out of it. If you go in aware of what you need to look for, it will speed up the process of finding the right space for you.

ERGONOMICS & DESIGN

Ergonomics is the field of design that looks at how things fit your body. You can easily replace the word ergonomics with comfort. One of the biggest mistakes people make

160

when looking at a coworking environment, is that they're driven more by style of the space (whether the space is chic and trendy or hipster) than they are by comfort.

Comfort is much more important in a coworking environment than style. One of the first things that people will instinctively, but not consciously, look for is natural light. It's a really important aspect of the coworking environment. Natural light has been linked to emotional wellbeing; it triggers the production of serotonin and regulates your circadian rhythms. It's a very important part of human health to be exposed to natural light, especially if you're in a northern or very southern part of the world where natural light is at a premium.

It's also worth considering what artificial illumination is within the space. Sometimes the light fittings chosen for eco reasons are not necessarily the best for one's health. A classic example of this would be fluorescent lighting. A lot of older fluorescent lighting will actually flicker at a range of around sixty hertz. For some people, that can trigger headaches and eyestrain and be very uncomfortable. LED lighting can be preferable because if it does flicker, it does so at a much higher frequency that doesn't seem to have the same effect on human comfort.

The space should not be lit in a homogeneous fashion. There should be areas that are bright for focus working and areas that are a bit dimmer for some reflective thinking or meditation. You need to look at task-based lighting around the space; spaces that have been well-thought-out for the user will have dedicated lighting for different tasks.

If you're touring a space, pause in a section that you like and then try and work out why you like it. If you're in an area of the space that you don't particularly like, pause there and try and work out why you don't like it. This practice will help guide your own individual preferences, because everybody has their own predilection as to the amount of light or brightness they like to work with. A well-designed space will provide for a spectrum of preferences.

Quite often people will walk into a coworking environment and see beautiful filament bulbs hanging from the ceiling by braided red or yellow or colourful cords and think, 'Wow, that's so trendy. It's really gorgeous.' However, while they throw off a lovely warm light, the quality of light from those bulbs is very poor. It's unfiltered direct light, it's not focused or diffused. If the light is coming from directly above you and it's unshielded, then you'll have very strong shadows. Those light sources will create significant glare if you're working off a laptop with a reflective screen.

The next thing to look for in a coworking environment is the physical working environment. Depending on the city and where you are in the world, people will make different provisions for space. A rule of thumb is generally the more expensive the real estate, the less space you'll be provided. Tour various spaces and get a sense of what the market average is for space. This will help you determine whether or not you're getting value for your money, in terms of the provision of space you've been allowed.

Keep in mind, however, that the quantity of space isn't as important as the quality of the space. This is where we lead into true ergonomics, which is the type of seating and desking that's provided. Within Collective Works, for example, we make desking available at several different heights to cater to people of all shapes and sizes. We offer standing desks at several different heights because somebody who's five-foot-two and somebody who's six-foot-eight will need very different desk heights.

Traditionally, a workspace will provide desking at a seventy-three-centimetre height, a European desk height, which may be inappropriate for people under five-foot-ten. If you're working in a space for a long period of time, a desk that's set at the wrong height for you is something that will cause back pain and potentially shoulder pain or a repetitive strain injury in your arms or shoulders.

The way to test various desk heights is to sit in the workspace and adjust it. See if you can get to the right posture, so that your femurs are at right angles to the floor, your feet are flat and your forearms are at right angles to the tabletop. Ask the host, 'Can the space provide any modifications for me?' The answer should be yes. At Collective Works, we have all of our tables on adjustable legs. If you ask that question and you get a blank face, then you're in a space that has invested far less heavily in the ergonomics and comfort of their members.

As you continue on your tour, be very aware of all of your senses. Notice the level of ambient noise. If you're a very gregarious, chatty person and you know you make noise or like listening to music when you're working and you walk into a workspace that is deathly silent, you may not be an ideal fit for that community.

Conversely, are people really chatty? Is there a lot happening, a lot of buzz? Buzz is great. Buzz makes you aware that everyone else is busy conducting activities; it creates the positive peer pressure that coworking is known for, which makes people more productive. You also want to be sure, however, that there are spots where you can go and hide away from that noise. Even the biggest extroverts have tasks to do where they need to get their head down.

If you're space shopping for a team, remember that everybody in your organisation is not like you. If you're part of a tech company, for example, there may be a sales side which is very chatty and engaged and spends a lot of time on the phone and there may be a development side which is very acoustically sensitive.

To give you an idea of how important this is, when we're onboarding new team members at Collective Works, we describe software developers as people that are effectively translating text into Latin in their heads; they're having to maintain a constant internal dialogue. They're thinking of what they want to do and how they are going to get there and they're translating it into a different language which is code - which is not a verbal language, which makes it even harder. Any acoustic or particularly verbal interruption to somebody who is doing that sort of internal monologue is incredibly disruptive. They'll lose their place in their work and it will take them several minutes to get back into what they're doing.

My team learned to handle these clients very carefully. They tend to be incredibly noise sensitive and need to be isolated away from other users who are not. Self-awareness of the kind of worker you are, or the kind of workers in your team, is a very big part of the ergonomics of design and comfort.

Other focuses of design and fit out include power, internet, heating, ventilation, air conditioning and sanitation. These characteristics are all essential to the mission of a coworking environment empowering its members.

HOW TO AVOID FALLING FOR STYLE OVER SUBSTANCE

It's a mistake to think that design is just about looking different, cutting edge or funky. The design of a coworking environment is what the users will **see**, feel and experience. In many ways, it is what differentiates a space in the market and determines whether or not it will have any customers.

Once again, this comes back to understanding what the user needs. Effective design is more about the user than aesthetics and occupancy planning. It starts with thinking about the types of spaces an entrepreneur needs to perform effectively.

At a minimum, a coworking environment needs both open, or 'we' space and closed, or 'me' space, where people can get away from their colleagues when they need to. However, this is a drastic oversimplification of human behaviour and display.

Here are some of the space types I have identified in my experience of running a collaborative workspace:

Working Space – Some people prefer a coffee-shop atmosphere for their working environment and find that the bustle and white noise of productivity really helps them concentrate. By contrast, reflective workspace is quiet and lower energy and is what people refer to when they say they want to get their head down or work from home.

Collaborative Space – The distinction between public and private spaces is more important in shared workspaces than single-occupancy ones. It is a question around who is party to a discussion and who is within earshot of a group discussion. If it is public, it is a discussion where users may be open to inviting third parties in, or at least won't object to their overhearing. If it is a confidential meeting, then it needs visual and acoustic separation. Collaboration isn't an on-going state – it is usually a short-term gathering or meeting, so this space is typically transient.

Social & Hospitality Space – In a traditional office, socializing and relationship building are what are referred to as 'water cooler' moments. They are parts of the day which are not directly related to productivity but are more to do with forming the bonds and relationships that enable business to take place. Social environments are important; there are peaks of use for morning coffee, lunch and afternoon tea and troughs for the rest of the day. Some of the best coworking spaces worldwide now include private restaurants and dining suites to allow members to entertain and impress.

Event Space – Event space is a more challenging form of social space because the demands are so exaggerated.

An event is by its very definition a short-term function. There are often exaggerated occupancy and guests and extraneous catering and technological demands. Event space is resource-heavy for short periods of time and then considerably vacant thereafter.

Single-Person Phone/Video Call Space – Traditionally, meeting rooms are used to achieve confidentiality for single-person calls, but generally the size of the room significantly exceeds the needs of a single person on a call. Using rooms in this fashion also limits the space's use for other important functions. Phone booths are a great solution but often expensive to implement. The challenge with this type of activity is how few people are involved and how far reaching the impact can be. One loud person on a Skype call can disturb an entire room of happy, productive people.

Group Call Space – Group calls are in many ways like any other meeting. They are highly productive and man-hour intensive, so ideal to hold in a high-value space like a meeting room. The only difference is the need for high quality telephony.

Physical Presentation/Pitching Space – Physical presentations used to be the mainstay of business and still play a very important role in business acquisition and retention. Wherever possible, important meetings are usually still held in person. Design in these spaces is essential, as business leaders want to make a positive impression.

Greeting/Impression Setting Space – Arrival and greeting are a very important part of the user experience, along with that of their clients. Thus, these spaces must be well-designed, without wasting space that could be used for other purposes.

Beyond the spaces required in a coworking environment, another element to consider is **flow**. Flow is the movement between spaces and the journey the environment carries a person through within a space. Flow significantly affects how effective the space is as a whole. I strongly believe that coworking environments should attempt to minimize travel time and corridor distances wherever possible.

To achieve all of these critical elements, at Collective Works we create ratios to empower our designers to generate enough revenue from the spaces we sell, as well as to create incredible experiential environments for our clients. One of these numbers includes designating a significant percentage of our floors to flexible, unbilled space. We do this to allow our clients room to move about, stretch and work in the fashion they like to. Why? Because this helps empower our clients by improving the quality of their work life and happier clients leads to better retention. While our clients don't know these percentages, they do know that these environments feel unlike any others in the market.

CURATION AND SECURITY

Collective Works has entry criteria, so even if you want to be a client, we won't necessarily take you. You've got to get through our background checks. To become a Collective

Works member, you have to not compete with an existing company. Second, you have to clear litigations checks, so you can't have any outstanding legal action against you, or a legal action against somebody else. Third, you've got to clear credit checks.

If we see people have excessive credit checks in their backgrounds, they're potentially in a tricky financial position, so we won't take them into the space without further investigation. We may ask for a reference, if we're unclear. You can circumvent some of these criteria if you're referred in by an existing member; the person who referred you would automatically serve as your reference.

Essentially, what we're trying to do with Collective Works is create a group of companies that are all playing at the same level - they are all high performers. We take curation seriously for a number of critical reasons.

This story represents one reason why: We once had an Australian gentleman walk into one of our spaces and want to sign up. He was almost too easy to sell. He was attended to by a new membership consultant on my team, so I assisted him with the sales process behind the scenes. My membership consultant went through the membership obligations with the visitor, who answered readily, 'Sure, no problem. Let's get started.'

The visitor left to get a coffee to allow us to process his application. I asked my new team member if he had yet completed his background checks. As he hadn't yet, we did the process together. I asked for the visitor's business card. He gave it to me and said, 'Oh, but he's registering for a different company.' I replied, 'Well, why is he giving you a card for a different company?' That was red flag number one. We pulled the corporate registration for the company he had asked to register and realised he wasn't a director or a shareholder of the business. That was red flag number two. I explained to my new team member that he can't register with a company he's not a director of - he doesn't have the right to. Then we started looking into him a little bit more.

We pulled all the legal and litigation checks from our system and couldn't find a lot on the guy. He had a pretty clean record in Singapore, but I couldn't shake the fact that he'd tried to register a company that he didn't have a right to register. To me, that's was a really dodgy thing to do. So, we started a news search against his full name and in minutes the first thing that came up was a bulletin from the Australian Security Exchange Commission. Massive red flag. This gentleman had run a fraudulent investment company in Australia and had lost millions of dollars of other people's money. He had been given a multi-year ban from owning and runing businesses in Australia and this would have extended to doing business in Singapore. Because of this, he was trying to register with us under a Hong Kong domiciled company and we started to suspect he was doing business under an entity that was being held on his behalf by others.

During his tour, he had shared that he'd been working in half a dozen other coworking environments in Singapore for various trial periods and it had become clear to me that none of them had checked him out. The potential for damage by putting somebody like that into a space is that people intrinsically trust other people who are in the same coworking environment. There's an assumption, 'You're like me, because we're in the same space.' People let their guard down. Really early on in my coworking business, we realised that we had a duty of care. Curating the community is a massive part of running a successful and safe coworking environment.

When we speak with potential clients and we tell them we do background checks, often they look at us like we're from outer space. We explain that if they were having a company come and work in their office, wouldn't they want to make sure they were legitimate? They reply something to the effect of, 'Well, that kind of makes sense.' In coworking, if I haven't met you before and we don't have a mutual connection in common, I'm going to check you out using social media, using Google, using all the tools I have at my disposal, so I can make a reasonable assessment that you're not trying to gain access to the space to harvest data, to steal things, or try and rip off my clients.

There was a case in Hong Kong a few years ago of a major coworking operator that entered the market and undercut all of the local operators by about 50 percent on their desk rates. Clients flocked to them, moving from other spaces in the surrounding areas because it was so cheap. Then this new budget coworking business hit a snag: Their membership rates were so low, that somebody saw an opportunity. A client signed up for a $100 hotdesking membership and then accessed the space out of hours on a weekend and took every piece of computer hardware they could carry. The estimates I hear were in the region of $50,000 worth of other people's computers.

Coworking environments are semi-public. You have to put some checks and balances in place. Companies interested in becoming members should ask about physical security and how the space is controlled from an access perspective. At Collective Works, none of our part-time members have access outside of our office hours of nine to five. For access outside of business hours, you need to be a dedicated member with a permanent desk, locker or office. You should also ask about data security: what security provisions are in place, how the network is segregated and who else you are sharing the network with. The space you choose should have a high-performance, well-configured network infrastructure.

All of the best coworking environments in the world are curated. The very best ones are heavily curated. To use some examples, there's a stunning space that started in New York called NeueHouse. It is a space built by designers for designers, for people in the fashion, media and arts industries. I believe they spent somewhere in the region of thirteen million dollars on their interior fit and the furniture is all exquisite. They have a beautiful, high quality restaurant. They have a co-op, or a membership board, that actually elects people into the space.

Not only is the space curated, there's a panel of members that actually decides who gets in. NeueHouse would be at the extreme end of curated space, but because they're curated, everybody within that space is more relevant to each other. Everybody within that space is approaching the world through a similar world lens; they believe their members will get more value with this approach.

The best coworking environments function a lot like the alumni associations or gentleman's clubs or professional networks which are valuable because everybody in the space is playing the same game. They are in the same league; they are peers. Going to a coworking environment with a degree of curation ensures that the community you're mixing with is relevant to you. What you will find is that people tend to do business with other businesses of equivalent or similar size to themselves.

When you're viewing a coworking environment, have a look at the kind of companies that are there. Look for signage in the space; the stage that these companies are at will tell you something. If the space, for example, has a multinational as part of that space, you know they're able to cater to later-stage businesses. The level of sophistication in that space will probably be a little bit higher.

If, as you go through the space, you notice a lot of bean bag chairs or a lot of members fresh out of university, that's going to tell you a lot about how that space is curated. If you see a hot mess of businesses with no real curation, that tells you something else - which is essentially that the space or the founder hasn't put a lot of time, thought or energy into understanding the membership and making sure that the space is relevant to them.

Once you have a good understanding of who you'd like to be around, finding a space that fits that bill is ideal. Making sure you're around people who are in the same stage of business, running their businesses in the same way as you and who are probably interested in similar things will greatly improve the impact of that space.

Ask if the space is targeting a particular niche or particular types of businesses. Ask if they're targeting any particular stage of business: Are they targeting startups? Are they targeting post-startup growth stage, multinational companies, or international companies? Be very cognizant of a coworking environment that can't answer those questions, or that answers those questions very generally, because it shows a lack of curation.

COMMUNITY

For years, real estate companies have made stable returns out of renting their office spaces, yet over those years they may never meet their customer. The client works with an agent to sign the lease and then subsequently pays their rent each month. There's no value add, there's no service, they're just gaining square footage - the lowest common denominator of a transaction.

Frankly, I think people have been making far too much money out of renting square footage for far too long and people are starting to expect more as a result. People now want a relationship with their transaction; in many ways, this is an anti-trend to the internet and anti-trend to globalization. Products and services have been dehumanized to such a point that people now want to buy a coffee from the little guy with the cart instead of from a big chain, because they'd like to feel a connection with their purchase.

At Collective Works, a lot of our members spend more time during the day with our staff than they spend with their loved ones. There's a real relationship that forms that you have to acknowledge; you can't avoid it. I've learned about marriages, I've learned about divorces, I've learned about kids, about affairs, about people dating other people and about business deals. We're intimately involved in our members' lives. Running a coworking environment is more like running a hotel than it is running an office, in terms of how much of peoples' lives we see. Failing to acknowledge that relationship will give you a really hollow coworking experience.

Half of coworking is the physical space, but the other half is the community within that space. It's very easy to quickly size up how lovely or how decadent an interior design or a physical environment is. It's much harder to quickly size up the quality and value of a community. In relation to the idea of curation, understanding the value of a community is understanding its value to you or to your business, not the value of the community itself.

The more relevant a community is to you, the more value it will have to you, which initially starts with self-reflection. What community are you looking to engage? If you're a large, multinational corporate working in finance, perhaps you're looking to approach the fintech startup community; there may be interesting developments there, which could be useful or synergistic to your own business.

Perhaps if you're a branch office and you're opening in a new country, you may be interested in working at a coworking environment with a large expat community, because members there will provide your team an element of home away from home. This environment may also give your team members access to people who have been where they're at and learned things the hard way and thus can give your members that extra support that they wouldn't have otherwise.

When you're viewing a space, the next question to ask is how does the space go about engaging their community? Ask them about events that the operator hosts. How often do they hold community get-togethers? What format are those get-togethers in and what are the takeaways? Can members initiate their own events? If they would be interested in doing so, what's the platform for doing that? The answers to these questions will give an awful lot of insight into the type of community present in the space.

The way spaces choose to engage their members is representative of how they view their members. A space that looks after early-stage businesses will have a lot of knowledge-sharing workshops and a lot of mentoring. Spaces that deal with more advanced communities will have a lot more networking, because the businesses will be at a stage where they are of value to each other. That mixing is very important.

Conversely, spaces that are dealing with even later-stage companies may bring in guest experts and very senior speakers on specific topics that deal with issues beyond startup and ideation. Again, the way a space treats its community is a reflection of the community itself. By taking a close look at the community, by understanding what you need and then by looking at how the space engages and excites their community, you'll get a very good sense of who's in the space and whether it's relevant to you.

TECHNOLOGY

Another aspect to look for in a coworking environment is its investment in IT. If my colleague Stephen tours a space looking for a team of bankers, this should be the first thing he asks about, because he's coming from a big corporate site. Under-investing in IT or having IT systems that are not equivalent to or exceeding the needs of the clients is a big problem.

I mentor other coworking operators and a few years ago there was a coworking environment about 500 metres from my first space. The operator called me because they were having problems with their internet. Their router kept locking up and their whole network would go down. It had gotten to the point where this breakdown was happening a few times a week. To attempt to assist them, I started by asking him what hardware they were using and he told me the model of router. It was an Asus home router. I said to him, 'That's the same router that I use in my apartment. The reason you're having problems with your internet connectivity is you're using a $300 router and you've got 100 people on it. You need a $5,000 router.' This is a mistake of being cheap for one thing, but frankly, it was also just ignorance on the part of the operator. He didn't know better.

In a world where we take wifi for granted and we all have it at home, it's important to remember two things. First, big wifi deployments are very different to domestic ones; they are highly complex and technical installations. Commercial wifi represents the dark art and science of getting enough wifi coverage to have good signal without having so much wifi coverage as to cause destructive interference. Second, just as a lot of people are not tech savvy, a lot of interior design companies and coworking operators are also not as savvy as they should be about this mission-critical infrastructure.

The next thing to look for in regard to technology is convenience. Are there proximate power points? Are there proximate data points? If you need to make a lot of Skype calls, or if you're a stockbroker or a trader or you're doing high quantities of information transfers, will the technological environment support those needs? If you're a graphic designer or videographer and you need to transfer files to the internet, having a wired connection is far superior to wifi. While it sounds obvious and it sounds sensible, you should never make assumptions about the provision of data and power in the space. The fundamental part of technology to have a look at is the internet connection and the way that the space delivers internet. With the internet running as the backbone of almost every business today, especially the kind of businesses that work in coworking environments, the quality of connectivity is not only essential, it's fundamental. Never assume the internet within a space is going to be as good as you want it to be. Always test it.

Have a look at the type and quality of the internet connection, or whether it's a dedicated IP address, or a dynamic IP address-based internet connection. Preferably, you want to look for fiber-optic based connections. Look at the top line download speed, but also at key attributes like latency. Latency is the number of milliseconds it takes to get a response from a network exchange; anything between two and five milliseconds is fantastic. Realistically, most spaces will be looking at a twenty to forty millisecond latency on their connections.

Ask who the internet service provider is for the space. If you're a business that does a lot of work with an international office, you might want to test the speed if you're connecting back over VPN to a foreign country. Wherever your company is based, you want to test the speed internationally on that connection. You may also want to consider asking the space if they operate a backup internet line. If they do, is it on the same provider or on a different provider? If there's any issue with an internet service provider, having a second line from a different provider gives you an extra level of security.

Additional good questions to ask are about bandwidth shaping; does the operator limit the amount of bandwidth each user gets in the network? If so, how are they limiting it? Find out if they're using VLANs, which is a virtual LAN or a virtual network which isolates different users on the network from each other, providing a greater level of network security. Questions like these put you into a completely different league as a client from the eyes of the space, but it also tells you important information about the levels of data security within the space.

Your business may need a physical telephone. The irony of smartphones is a lot of smartphones now aren't very good for making phone calls. Find out if the space has a telephone system. If your company uses Salesforce or an online phone system that's centralised, or maybe even Microsoft phone systems or Google phone systems, a space may not allow you to bring that system in if it competes with their existing phone network. Particularly if you're a multinational provider where it's very likely that you'll have some enterprise grade phone systems, these are important things to know before subscribing to the coworking environment.

Furthermore, you want to make sure the space has suitable provisions for firewalls and rack space in server rooms and find out whether their server rooms are air-conditioned or not. Make sure they have the correct provisions of meeting room equipment to have conference calls and video conferencing. Is their technology compatible with the hardware and software systems that you use?

One of the final things to consider when looking at technology in a coworking environment, is whether the space has any strategic partnerships with service providers you use or may be interested in using. A lot of big technology companies are very interested in working with coworking spaces. Google, Microsoft and Amazon Web Services have all set up relationships with coworking environments which will give you a reduced price.

Those relationships could save your business hundreds of dollars a year per user, if they're used correctly. Those strategic relationships can be a very valuable addition to a coworking environment and are typically unavailable to small businesses or branch offices operating independently of these large aggregate spaces.

RESPONSIBILITY

As a coworking operator, something I hammer into my team when they start is that we have a duty of care. Most of our customers come to our space and take for granted that we have the right chairs, the right tables, the right internet connection for them and that we're going to have the correct provision. They trust us to take care of all of those needs. These companies rely on us to run their businesses and if we have an internet outage or our space is making somebody less effective, their business is less productive. The ripple effect of what we do is quite significant; not enough coworking environments really acknowledge that duty of care.

It's important that you subscribe to a coworking environment that understands the gravitas and the responsibility that comes with providing space for dozens or hundreds of businesses. What you want to look at is how slick is their operation? How organized are they? If they make an appointment, do they keep it on time? If there's someone expecting you when you arrive, that is a sign that the space has systems and processes in place.

In an emerging industry like coworking, new spaces are opening every day. Spaces under three years old know little about the responsibility that comes with a coworking environment, because they haven't been around long enough to encounter major customer service failings, to learn from them and put proper systems and processes in place. Especially for these newer companies, consider the following questions: Do they take what they're doing seriously? Is the space their primary focus, or is it a sideline business? Again, all of those answers will inform the caliber of the space and the approach the space takes and you'll get hints and clues as you go through the space.

The number of years in operation also affects the quantity and diversity of a space's client base. The more companies and countries and industries the space has dealt with, the better their operating processes are going to be, because they've had to deal with a huge spectrum of environments. Such processes might include the understanding that they have a responsibility to provide disabled access, bicycle parking, backup internet and other fundamental things that corporates and MNCs already know about and perhaps take for granted.

While coworking can be a very exciting and diverse and dynamic environment for the employees of multinational companies to work in, it's important to remember that a lot of these spaces are new and may not have learned a lot of the life lessons that other businesses have learned. Getting a gauge of that sense of responsibility, that sense of ownership over space and sense of maturity that a space brings to their operations is very important and will ensure that you choose a partner that's successful for a longer-term relationship.

UNDERSTANDING OF THE MARKET

The kind of working space a computer programmer needs and the kind of space a designer needs are quite different. Every industry has its own unique needs and what sets good coworking offices apart from others is their ability to cater to those different needs. If you asked the owners of a traditional serviced office who they cater to, their reply would be something like, 'global business people.' That is a wonderful catchall phrase that tells you very little about what people do, how they function or even how they earn an income.

My brother and I are both global business people. Prior to starting my coworking environment, I ran a public relations and branding studio. My brother is a highly-educated banker who manages financial trading products for billion-dollar corporations. Yes, we are both international business people, but my needs as a creative business owner with just a handful of high-net-worth clients and his as a financial business with a portfolio of some of the world's largest companies couldn't be more different.

Think for a moment about the confidentiality demands on each of us. How about the hours we work, the way we dress and the meetings we hold? I use Skype, my brother uses Cisco Telepresence. If we were both looking for office space, it would be unlikely that the same space would be able to cater to both of us equally well.

Let's look at another example. One of my clients was an internet startup restaurant booking app called Chope. Chope is a classic work hard, play hard startup company. Very few of their team members would come to the office before 10 a.m., but they would work long past midnight most days. They have a young staff and follow the time-shifted pattern of late nights and late mornings. This means their office needs to be accessible late into the evening.

Like many businesses nowadays, Chope's system runs in the cloud, not onsite. This is great from a business interruption perspective. However, it also means their office needs a bulletproof connection to that cloud. Not being able to contact the mother ship has a serious business impact for the company. Knowing what we know about their work habits, we know we need an internet service provider that doesn't perform maintenance at midnight – we need one that performs maintenance at 5 a.m.

Chope also has two distinct working styles due to their two core divisions – frontend sales and backend programming and support teams. Naturally, these teams conduct business in different ways. The sales team is primarily out of the office, spending their days visiting clients. When they are in the office they are loud, social and often on the phone. Sales teams are the life of the party, so they need space to express themselves.

At the other end of the spectrum, the programming employees at Chope are quiet, focused and rather intense. Imagine how it feels to be concentrating constantly for eight hours a day. Their job is to solve complex equations in their heads, like translating an encyclopaedia into a different language. This work requires an in-depth, internal monologue to juggle information and convert it. Naturally, these are people who are very sensitive to noise and distractions.

With this short example, we have already found two different and distinct working styles that have polar opposite needs from their environment. One needs a podium, the other needs a cocoon. By knowing this company's working style, I can see how important it is that these two teams are kept separate because their working styles are not only different but very disruptive to each other. A coworking environment needs to understand their market in order to empower them.

CHAPTER NINE TAKEAWAYS

▶ In order to determine if a coworking environment suits the needs of your business, you're going to need not only a tour but an actual test drive.

▶ The key criteria you should look at include: Ergonomics (comfort and usability of the space);

▶ Design (the environment should include work space, collaborative space, social space, space to make both private and group phone calls, presentation space and greeting space);

▶ Curation (physical security and how the space is controlled from an access perspective);

▶ Community (What community are you looking to engage? How does the space go about engaging their community?);

▶ Technology (type and quality of internet connection, power points, etc.);

▶ Responsibility (sense of ownership the company has over the space)

▶ A coworking environment needs to understand their market in order to empower them. Every industry has its own unique needs and what sets coworking offices apart from serviced offices is their ability to cater to those needs.

COWORKING REBELLION

What about the future of coworking? If coworking really is a sign of deep seated dissatisfaction with our physical world, how is it going to affect our environment? In this chapter we will explore some of the potential ways coworking is evolving our cities and the space around us to right size our physical environment and our ideological one.

INTEGRATED BUILDINGS

There was a point in history where an office tower was simply an office tower. It contained primarily or exclusively office space with nothing else. As time went on, real estate developers saw an opportunity to add ground floor amenities, coffee shops and restaurants for the residents of these buildings, which made the buildings more

THE EVOLUTION OF BUILDING ECOSYSTEMS OVER TIME

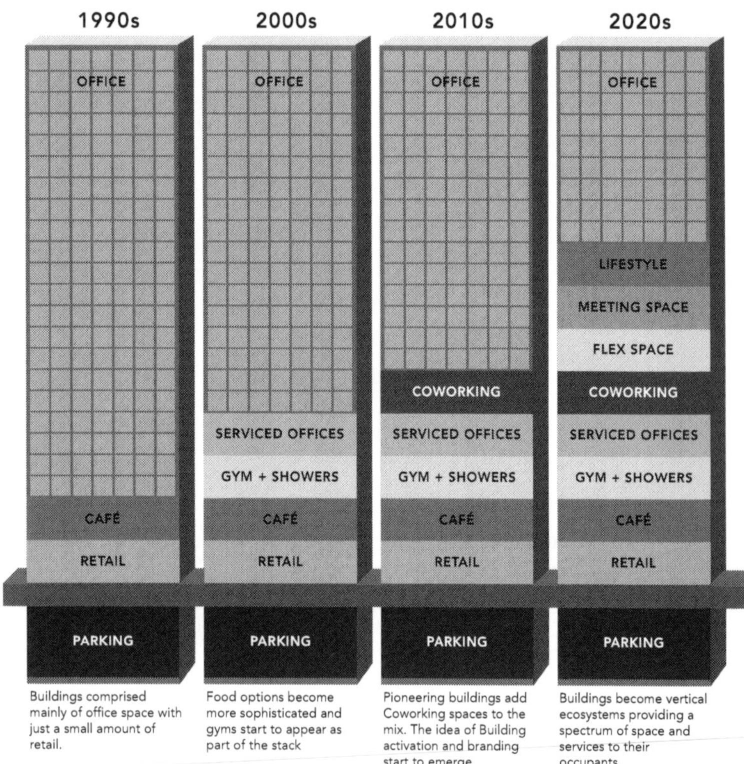

Buildings comprised mainly of office space with just a small amount of retail.

Food options become more sophisticated and gyms start to appear as part of the stack

Pioneering buildings add Coworking spaces to the mix. The idea of Building activation and branding start to emerge

Buildings become vertical ecosystems providing a spectrum of space and services to their occupants.

relevant to the tenants. This model offered convenience and it made use of inefficient or inflexible space.

As trends evolved in the 2000s, developers started looking at buildings as almost a sandwich. The ground floor would typically have food, coffee and a refreshment presence. Perhaps there would be an integrated gym or parking in the building and a residential or hospitality hotel component stacked with offices.

The idea of this multifunction, 'sandwich' ecosystem evolved to what we're looking at now - which is essentially the Holy Grail of an integrated building. By 'integrated building,' I'm referring to a building that acts as an ecosystem that in some way provides a function for the members or occupants of that building to move fluidly between services. This structure provides flexibility, making the tenants' physical space more relevant to them.

With increased pressures on physical workspace and transport within global megacities, integrated buildings make more and more sense. These buildings require people to travel less and allow them to achieve more when they're in one location.

To accomplish those goals, developers have to make sure they're not putting barriers in people's ways. If they need one supplier for food and beverage, one supplier for the office space, one supplier for the fitness environment, one supplier for hospitality or the wellness environment and one supplier for a residential component...it really erodes the value proposition and the ease of use for the client because these systems don't integrate. At every point, they're building unique relationships without a full and complete understanding of the person as a whole.

As we've discussed earlier, one of the real value propositions of coworking is a fluent understanding of the client and a tailored solution for their needs. The more coworking environments know about their members, the better they can service them and the better they can provide them with a comprehensive working and living environment. The added value achieved with this model can be compared to the advantage of having a personal assistant over outsourcing each task to different suppliers.

Having a knowledge base in all of these areas really streamlines the relationship between company and client and creates a single point of contact. While the idea of an integrated building is fantastic, the execution of it is a nightmare. I don't know of a multi-occupant building yet worldwide to have actually achieved that level of integration - but it's coming.

To achieve the next level of an integrated building, the introduction of a coworking environment as part of the building stack is required. This model requires a high-rise or super-high-rise building, because to go to this level of integration warrants a large enough target scale. So, let's consider buildings that are fifty stories or higher and a million square feet plus, that have several thousand occupants. I'll use a building in Singapore as an example.

Collective Works has recently joint ventured with CapitaLand Singapore on exactly those concepts. As a founder and builder of coworking environments, I have become really interested in the idea of an integrated building, or a vertical ecosystem. I've also become very interested in how they can differentiate themselves and make themselves more relevant to a new generation of working professional.

While the earliest models of integrated buildings began as stacks of buildings with sandwiches of services, they were missing an element that actually tied the whole centre together. I'll use Capital Tower, which is the fifth tallest building in Singapore, as an example.

The building contains a ground floor with a Starbucks and a suite of beautiful restaurants ranging from salad bars to sushi. It has seven floors of parking. It has its own Fitness First, a large, beautiful gym with a swimming pool. It has a 240-seat auditorium and a 60-seat meeting room. It even has dentists and medical facilities, with a general practitioner and a dermatologist. Thirty-six floors up in the air, it has a coffee shop in the sky on the major transfer floor. Though the owner did a fantastic job of providing a stack of services, there is very little actually tying those services together. There is no focal point for community in that centre.

While I would not say Collective Works has been able to achieve an integrated building at this stage, it is something that we're working towards. I think the future of coworking involves looking at partnerships between community builders and physical asset holders. The idea is to create engagement of the individual, as opposed to engagement on a macro, corporate level - to deliver a truly remarkable experience for that person.

Imagine a building where you show up for work in the morning and the whole building knows who you are. You have a key, perhaps it's not physical and the whole experience is powered by facial recognition. That key gets you into the gym, opens your locker, operates the turnstiles for the security of the building and gets you into your office. That same key lets you use the vending machines to get your coffee, allows you to access meeting rooms, lets you buy food from any retailer in the building by presenting your card and it can log you into your company's network and phone system at any point in the building.

To have that kind of fluid relationship that wove through an entire building would create such a delightful working environment for people. As populations increase and cities become more competitive, the idea of these integrated buildings becomes more and more important. For an urban megacity, this model is really the gold star aspiration for the future of coworking.

Could we create a building that was so fully integrated, that it actually owned the full working life of somebody? Or maybe even their complete lifecycle, if we went as far as co-living? Could we provide the necessary services all the way through from residential through commercial and completely take away the need for that person to own a physical space? Could they simply operate their full life as a subscription, making them in effect completely unattached, untethered and able to go wherever they like?

It's an interesting mind game and an intriguing philosophy for the future. In many ways, we're already looking at the end of owning. From music services to cars, our culture is moving towards a subscription model.

The idea of owning a home is still very much engrained in our collective psyche. I think people aspire in much the same way to own or rent their own business space. Quite a prominent real estate investor in the U.K. visited recently and said that the biggest mistake he ever made in his entire financial career was buying his first home when he was thirty years old. Owning a home that one can't afford and paying into a mortgage is a destructive financial cycle. Also, with the exponential population growth the world is experiencing, it's unrealistic for everybody to expect to own their own home.

However, it doesn't mean we don't have enough space. All it means is that the pressure on physical space will become so high that the costs will become prohibitive. We're already seeing that problem in cities like Singapore or Hong Kong and Tokyo. Such cities are excellent places to explore this modern, integrated building model.

THE SASSIFICATION OF REAL ESTATE — HARDWARE MADE FLEXIBLE

When we strip away all of the social references of coworking and the ideas of hospitality and community, at its very core coworking is Real-Estate-as-a-Service, or Environment-as-a-Service. Effectively, what it's done is taken something that would have been a fixed operating overhead for most businesses and turned it into the equivalent of a software subscription that can be turned on and off.

In the past, everyone in business had copies of Microsoft Office software; now, everyone is moving over to the cloud-based Office365. In effect, we pay slightly more for the Software-as-a-Service subscription than we did for Microsoft Office, but we get the latest version of the software, all the security updates and we don't have to go to the store and buy a new copy. Coworking, or Real Estate-as-a-Service, is very much the same; there are a lot of added benefits. It's an environment that's continually improving, updating and progressing. Naturally, there is a cost premium for that.

However, the big difference in Real-Estate-as-a-Service and Software-as-a-Service is the base cost of providing the service. In real estate, the basic overheads are quite high, which means coworking is fundamentally a margin business. Coworking environments exploit the inefficiency in current office planning and make their profits in the margin of waste that companies normally have in commercial space. This model means that coworking environments need to run full and be well-designed for them to be successful and profitable.

The coworking industry, at least in its early days, is one that's been plagued by low profitability. In the Deskmag annual coworking survey in 2016, 45 percent of the spaces surveyed worldwide were not profitable – they were either break even or were losing money. But we have to consider that the average size of a coworking environment worldwide at the time consisted of approximately fifty members, which is very small. So, the challenge of profitability was one of critical mass.

We're currently seeing a trend in coworking towards mega space or ultra-large spaces, because they have to operate on a scale that's large enough for the margins to make sense. With a slim margin, the operator needs scale. In the early days of coworking, the spaces were mainly under 5,000 square feet. Over the past few years, we've seen 10,000 square feet become the new 5,000 square feet and now 20,000 square feet has become the new 10,000 square feet. WeWork, one of the most famous coworking operators, regularly opens spaces in the 70,000 to 100,000 square-foot-scale, if not larger.

What we're seeing now is the emergence of mega-operators; by using scale on that margin, coworking environments make enough money to continue to fund their growth and build more spaces on scale. The advantage of building on scale is multi-fold. Apart from making more money, building on scale actually improves design efficiency, because less space is handed over to corridors and duplication. Large floor plan buildings actually provide a more efficient layout, which means there is more room left over to create common space and space for ping-pong tables, nap rooms, collaborative zones and kitchens and cafes and all the lovely luxuries that people like to think of in coworking environments that make them so enticing.

With the emergence of large-scale spaces, what we're seeing is effectively the planned obsolescence or the forced redundancy of small coworking environments. These small spaces cannot compete with the shine factor of a space on scale, because they can't afford to carve up such generous proportions to non-productive or ancillary uses.

When we look at a market like Singapore, which at the time of publishing in 2018 is going through a coworking transformation, by my count Singapore currently has over 120 spaces with over twenty multisite operators. However, I would forecast in the next two years, the number of operators will begin to consolidate to something closer to five significant operators. The driving factors for this shift are the forced obsolescence of smaller space and the generous funding flowing into the market from the U.S. and China. Those conditions force operator growth that outpaces market demand and efficiencies of scale for the larger operators, which combined with their robust balance sheets allow them to run with the narrowest margins in the industry and undercut the smaller home-grown spaces. We've already started to see this impact on smaller and less efficient spaces that physically no longer make enough profit to be sustainable.

Anybody that's been in business long enough will tell you that you need a certain degree of profitability to maintain sustainability, but you also need to have a business that can ride through different economic times. A lot of the coworking environments that have been built to date were built in a rising market; they were built in an expansive period of freelance growth, in a recovery period from the global financial crisis and they were built in a period with depressed real estate overheads.

As the world economies recover and rental rates recover as well, the models of some of these spaces are effectively no longer viable. That means coworking as we know it today is still very much a nascent version of the end product. What we're going to see more of are large-scale spaces with phenomenal facilities. The challenge that model creates is maintaining what I call human scale - a scale where people feel comfortable and are still able to access and relate to the community on a personal level and avoid that feeling of an airport lounge.

One of the ironic stories from the Real-Estate-as-a-Service industry is that for years, many of the serviced offices - Regus and the like - were aspiring to create the feeling of an airport lounge in an office. That's the antithesis of what a coworking environment is trying to do. If you've ever spent time in an airport lounge, while they're beautiful and well-appointed, no one actually speaks to each other. People actually try to avoid each other. Partly, that behaviour is due to the transient nature of airport lounge clientele; you don't know who these people are and you will most likely never see them again. But the scale and size of airports alone contributes to making these spaces very impersonal. There's the dilemma: the future of coworking is definitely big and driven primarily by economic factors but the challenge will be to keep the intimacy and person connection of small.

HYPER NICHING — AGGREGATE BUSINESSES

Coworking environments should have a really thorough idea of who the end-user of the coworking environment actually is. The best coworking environments in the world are focused and the very best are hyper niched.

One of my favourite hyper-niche coworking environments is just outside of New York. It's a coworking environment built for recording artists. The target demographic for the space is musicians, or aspirational musicians. The space includes a recording studio with all of the equipment, recording decks and soundproof booths that a recording musician would need, but it is structured in a way to make it accessible to the members.

Recording studio space is normally prohibitively expensive and very difficult to access on a regular basis. By crowdsourcing the project, the company was able to create a recording environment that is a lot more accessible, a lot more affordable and that caters to the needs of their demographic. The space has no relevance to anybody outside of recording musicians. Somebody in finance, for example, would find very little benefit to joining that space; the synergies, the connections and the type of people using that space would have very little resemblance.

The need for hyper niching in coworking is driven by the awareness that we choose to hyper niche in life. Consider any successful company - let's take J.P. Morgan, for example. J.P. Morgan is a global investment bank. I run a coworking environment in the same building as their Singapore office. The company consists of an incredibly chic set of bankers who dress very particularly for work. They wear suits, they wear Prada shoes, they carry beautiful bags; they are truly suited and booted. There's a J.P. Morgan look to this J.P. Morgan set.

The brand and what it means to work for J.P. Morgan is captured by the employees; it is extremely premium, it is very educated and it is very polished. The company culture is such that their employees fit their mould; they are representative of the brand and therefore, will succeed better in that organisation if they share a common goal, attitude and focus. That brand strategy makes for a very successful company - having people that are unified and highly syncronised working towards a common goal.

What makes J.P. Morgan an interesting example of a hyper-niched financial institution is not only the fact that they have a really clear aesthetic, but that they have such a defined aesthetic that they actually forgot it. In 2016, they issued a worldwide memo that caused a huge consternation: They relaxed their aesthetic to "business casual". They told a demographic of men that wore precision suits and ladies in power stilettos with designer handbags that it was okay to come to work in business casual.

In my opinion as an outsider, the people that work for J.P. Morgan appreciate, respect and enjoy their aesthetic. It's part and parcel to who they are and it's a sign of their perfectionism and excellence in the way they look and how they execute. To parody coworking, understanding whether a coworking operator focuses on a demographic that wears jeans or a three-piece suit is key to building the right space for the right market in the right place.

We ran into a really interesting dilemma with one of our new coworking environments. In 2016, we opened

Collective Works in a very prestigious building in Singapore called Capital Tower. Singapore is the home of branded buildings. As discussed earlier, a branded building is a building with a unique aesthetic, look and feel. Capital Tower actually has its own dress code. While it's a fifty-two-story building with more than seven hundred thousand net lettable square feet, it only had thirteen tenants - including J.P. Morgan and other very sophisticated, blue-chip businesses and governmental organisations with very formal and professional outlooks on the world.

When we opened Collective Works Capital Tower, some of the other companies in the building were genuinely concerned that we were going to be transplanting hoodie-wearing, Bermuda short and flip-flop techie types into their ivory tower. The fears were misplaced, because our coworking environment had a really clear idea of the kind of company and the kind of person that would aspire to work in a building that looked, felt and smelled the way that Capital Tower does. Companies attracted to this location see themselves as future blue chips and they look and behave very much the same way. Just because people belong to a small company doesn't mean they wear Bermuda shorts.

With coworking environments becoming effectively aggregate businesses - environments or crossroads of commerce where small businesses gather to interact with each other - it only makes sense to make these environments tailored. The spaces should mean something; they should create an environment that stands for something so that the people aggregating and collecting in these environments are more relevant to each other.

Coworking started very much on a theme of 'everybody's invited.' The earliest coworking environments were open to every culture, creed and industry. While this policy presents a beautiful and idealistic view of the world, it limits in many ways the benefits that people offer to each other.

There are forums where an everybody's-invited approach makes sense. The perfect example is a destination coworking environment in Bali, because the clientele in Bali are escaping their normal lives. There's a disproportionate number of people who go to Bali to find themselves, to take a step back from life and discover something new. In that context, an eclectic mix of web designers, artists and financiers under one roof makes complete sense. In the normal run of business, where people are stable and comfortable and performing in a role, such an environment is not creative or productive - it would actually be disruptive: context is important to whether a community focus will be successful.

To give another example, in Singapore we've recently seen the opening of a 30,000-square-foot fintech space. To many people, it would be counter-intuitive to put a density of similar businesses in such a tightly-knit industry together, but the benefits to the companies that have chosen to take part in the space far outweigh the risks and the competition. We need to remember we have entered a new era of a collaborative economy and many believe we can achieve more collectively than we can alone.

This practice is driven by a very interesting change in perception; we're now in the generation of collaboration. We have a generation of workers that believe they can achieve more by sharing ideas and resources than by behaving the way their parents did in the '70s and '80s in the era of corporate secrecy, privacy and corporate espionage.

In Singapore, there is a coworking environment just for social enterprise; their focus is exclusively on social need. There's another space called Hackerspace, which is just about tech and programming. And for a time there was a wonderful space called Woolf Works, designed exclusively as a place of refuge for women to write and create and escape from their daily lives. Not all of these spaces are commercially successful because the economic dynamics of coworking remain unchanged – a market of sufficient critical mass is needed to support the space. However, these niche spaces are magical environments and they have a magnetism and stickiness and brand power that is dramatically larger than their modest size.

At the moment, hyper niching is happening on a very small scale - small physical spaces with perhaps only twenty members. What we have yet to see are hyper-niched coworking environments being extended to large-scale spaces, where they actually make an impact from a business perspective. Solving a hyper-niche environment at scale is key to developing future branded real estate where the culture and community matches the physical construction.

AGGREGATOR OF EXPERTISE

I view coworking environments as aggregators that consolidate smaller teams with pockets of expertise into something far more meaningful and impactful. There are some phenomenal supporting statistics that came out of Europe a few years ago. There was a study done which showed that businesses that started operations in a coworking environment were 30 percent less likely to fail than businesses that tried to go it alone.

You may have heard the statistic that 80 to 90 percent of all small businesses fail before they reach three years old. However, the statistic most people have not heard is that of the remaining businesses, 80 to 90 percent fail every year thereafter. The small businesses that sustain themselves for over five years are the 10 percent, of the 10 percent, of the 10 percent. That, unfortunately, is not the best invitation to encourage small business. At the same time, small business is an enormously powerful and important driving force in the world economy and in future development.

So, what drives that 30 percent increase in success for small businesses that start life in coworking environments? Part of the driving force is camaraderie; it eliminates isolation. If you come from a large corporate culture and start a small business, you will quickly realise you have done so in isolation from the support system of knowledge and expertise you are used to. You lose the ability to simply tap somebody on the shoulder and ask, 'What do you think about this?'

Human beings are essentially social people. Small business is an environment where people are pushed beyond their comfort zones. They're forced to ideate. They're forced to innovate. They're forced to experiment and continually learn. However, you can only learn when you have people or resources to learn from. The beauty of a coworking environment is that it provides access to experience, resources and expertise across the diverse makeup of its membership base.

Using Collective Works as an example, you could be working in a centre with 300 or 400 people who have experience across every industry and every walk of life. If you need to speak with someone about marketing, you could speak to one of our public relations or branding agents. If you need to speak to somebody about finance or funding, you could speak to a business that advises startups, or one of our venture capitalists. By aggregating, or collecting small businesses with segmental focus, what coworking environments actually do is simulate all of the knowledge resources of a large organisation.

If we look at a large company, regardless of the industry, they typically segment into a particular function that every business requires to function: human resources, finance, customer service, product delivery, operations and information technology. A well-curated coworking environment will have representation in each of these areas, so that somebody within that space has access to that knowledge or resource without necessarily taking on the overhead.

Let me give an example. Before I started Collective Works, I came up with a business called the Creative Collective. The concept for Creative Collective follows the framework I outlined in my coworking methodology. It's mission driven, collaborative, creative and effective. The concept came from my experience of having previously owned a public relations and branding agency. From time to time, I needed to hire accountants, lawyers, videographers, illustrators, graphic designers, web designers and computer programmers to deliver the services that I sold to my clients.

I used to describe my business as an accordion business; it would expand when we had a lot of work or a complex project and it would contract when we completed the project and I no longer needed the services of those freelancers. When we look at the global trend towards freelance and entrepreneurship and the global trend towards autonomous working, we see a larger workforce that wants to work flexibly, to choose the way that they work and the projects that they work on.

The question I asked myself was, what would happen if we aggregated all of those areas of expertise under one roof? What would happen if we made a crowd-sourced marketing agency? We would have a freelance videographer, web designer, a group of illustrators and a group of graphic designers, all centralised around a core team of client management. The talent would own the agency and the space could provide the service of attracting and bringing in business and the administration of work between members or the participants of this creative, collaborative community.

It was an incredibly powerful idea, potentially transformative for the creative industries, but quite frankly, it was a little bit ahead of its time. What I realised very quickly was that there was a need beyond just the creative industries to provide some form of aggregator. There was a need for a form of infrastructure and maybe even a support system to allow small teams to maintain the profitability and lean advantages of being small, but to still be sustainable.

Aggregators address a number of the challenges faced by small teams, be they small businesses or just offshoots of larger organisations. Small teams experience 'keyman risk.' If one person in a team falls sick, a significant percentage of the company is missing. That in itself presents quite an interesting challenge for the longevity and sustainability of small business. While there are a lot of great things about operating small businesses, namely speed, efficiency, autonomy, lean operating models and a lack of waste, there are conversely a number of challenges: point risk, lack of scalability, access to knowledge, access to resources. Those are problems that have been traditionally solved by businesses getting larger, by employing more people and essentially ceasing to be small businesses.

All that being said, small businesses in many ways are beautiful. So much so that it has become fashionable for large organisations to seek to recreate the culture and the dynamics that naturally occur in smaller ones. Small companies have become the focal point for research and development for many large organisations, which is driving the trend we've seen of medium-sized companies acquiring small companies with innovative tech and innovative ideas. It's much cheaper for a small company to experiment. In fact, it's much cheaper for a small company to fail. That's part of the reason why small business has achieved so many great things. Small companies can and do achieve great things and if we create the right infrastructure around them then small business may well become an improved, high efficiency, higher engagement operating model.

The challenge we're presented with in the future of small business is how do we make small sustainable? How do we de-risk small? How do we make small as scalable and sustainable as being large without losing the benefits of being small? The answer is to aggregate them. Aggregating businesses is an interesting challenge. Typically, businesses have been aggregated using roll ups, mergers and corporate structuring - never societally or relationally linked as communities. Unfortunately, by merging or rolling up small businesses, you often break what fundamentally makes them successful.

Up until now, we haven't had a particularly successful way of making small businesses more sustainable, less susceptible to point risks and more resilient without breaking what made them special. Coworking environments provide an incredible canvas, an incredible platform for small business. Moreover, it has been statistically proven that coworking environments reduce small business mortality and increase employee satisfaction and engagement.

INTERFACE FOR MNCs

Traditionally, a multinational company is unlikely to work with a small to medium enterprise (SME). As discussed earlier, a small to medium-sized business isn't scalable enough to service multinationals at scale. However, just because historically there hasn't been a platform for this kind of partnership to work doesn't mean that such partnerships shouldn't happen. With the right interface it does make sense for a MNC to engage with SMEs and PLRDs. These smaller teams can represent safe sandboxes for experimentation and agile working that are not possible inside highly regulated MNC environments. Coworking spaces, particularly segmented ones, are starting to play the role of aggregator, curator and an interface for corporations. And, these large companies are starting to see the benefit of engaging with aggregators that have clearly defined missions.

When small businesses are presented in aggregate, it makes sense for a MNC to find a small business to work with, knowing that they have the support structure of a coworking environment. For example, it makes sense for a bank to approach a coworking environment aggregator that has a niche of fintech. The bank is far more likely to achieve a result, because the company is dealing with multiple people in one space. If help is needed, they can access an immediately proximate resource from within the coworking environment.

That support structure offers sustainability. The fact that a business has already been able to get itself into a coworking environment and afford the overheads and costs therein, already acts as a bit of a clearinghouse. It proves that the company is already a more sustainable business than a business that's working from home or from a garage.

Looking into the future, it's understood that multinational companies aren't going away. Our society still requires big industrial companies, big pharmaceutical companies and big manufacturing companies. The challenge now is that while we have all of the big companies that we need, but we don't have all of the small companies pushing the envelope. However, it's very difficult for a micro-level company to engage with a macro-level company without an interface in between. The coworking corporation, or an aggregate, is an ideal conduit for that mechanism that provides inordinate benefit to both the SME and the MNC.

ROBOTS AND ARTIFICIAL INTELLIGENCE - THE END OF MENIAL LABOUR

Another aspect to consider in regard to the future of coworking is understanding that we are about to use science and technology to replace many aspects of business. Menial work will be automated due to the advent of artificial intelligence and robotics. This shift should free people up to work on aspects of higher evolution, ideation and thinking. Ideally, it should move the world forward, instead of seeking to maintain the status quo. Since we have established that creativity, flexibility, play, experimentation and risk are all elements that work better in small teams, that environment is very important to maintain.

The Savioke Relay Robot is a very cute, 92 cm-high service robot designed for hospitality environments. Relay's primary function is to deliver items from A to B. "He" connects into a phone system; can call the lift when he needs to go between floors. He can be used in a coworking space to deliver mail or room service to each of the studios within a space. If a customer wants a soft drink or a bar of chocolate, Relay can take care of that. Relay will make his way to the room you tell him to go to, call the phone of the person in that room and tell him or her that he's there with a delivery. The person will type a code into his or her iPad face and be able to retrieve the items from Relay. When he's done, Relay goes back and charges himself until you need him again.

With Relay, automating fundamentally repetitive functions frees up your team to have discussions, provide services and conduct the personal tasks that cannot be automated. I see robotics as the end of menial work, the end of repetition and the end of what is often called 'busy work' - moving things from A to B, responding to emails and so forth.

I know of a coworking environment in Australia that uses an artificial intelligence (AI) to book tours and client meetings. Essentially, you copy the AI on an email and ask him to book an appointment. The AI will have a discussion with the person who needs to book a meeting with you and will find the appropriate time in both calendars.

Any company can afford to pay $50 per month to use one of the artificial intelligence services on the internet. Technology has put a phenomenal amount of power in the hands of business leaders, in a sustainable and affordable way. Businesses of any size can effectively achieve today what used to only be available to multinationals. This shift has really upset the power dynamic of business.

We're entering a very interesting time in the world. A time of artificial intelligence, a time of automation and a time where even more people will be displaced, potentially more than were in the global financial crisis. These people will have to find other ways to spend their time and other ways to earn their livelihood, but at the same time, what an interesting and wonderful opportunity this era presents. What if everybody could do what they loved doing, instead of doing menial tasks just to earn a wage? While I admit it is an idealized view of the world, it is one that may not be so unrealistic in the near future, or in the 2025 that is being envisioned.

GLOBAL COHESION — THE NEED FOR INTERNATIONAL STANDARDS

In a 2017 forecast by Emergent Research in Partnership with GCUC, the coworking movement is forecast to reach over 5.1 million members and 31,000 spaces across the globe by 2022. These spaces include hobby space, social spaces and pro spaces. However, with the movement expected to continue its meteoric rise, it will need better organisational support from broad associations that can better advocate for workers and owners with local, state and federal governments.

There are a number of prominent leaders on behalf of the movement, but they are generally focused on one geographic location. There are no worldwide or continental organisations to support the movement. To take North America as an example, the continent has nine collectives, or organisations supporting the coworking movement. However, a number of these organisations are coalitions or alliances of a number of coworking environments that help support each other in a specific city. Examples include Coworking Toronto, Denver Coworks and the Texas Code Collective.

By contrast, the LExC (League of Extraordinary Coworking Spaces) and COSHARE are collectives of coworking environment owners from across the U.S. that are looking to become national organisations that represent coworking owners.

In order to grow, the coworking environment requires a cohesive network of organisations that can advocate for both coworking environment owners and members within specific cities and countries and on a global scale. As yet, the coverage is very thin to non-existent and the movement may be suffering as a result of that loose cohesion.

CHAPTER TEN TAKEAWAYS

▶ Integrated buildings (buildings that act as an ecosystem that in some way provides a function for the members or occupants of that building to move fluidly between services) could be a future standard for coworking environments.

▶ A trend in coworking is taking place towards mega space or ultra-large spaces, because coworking environments have to operate on a scale that's large enough for the margins to make sense. These large-scale spaces will have phenomenal facilities,

▶ Coworking environments will continuously move toward hyper-niching. As environments or crossroads of commerce where small businesses gather to trade and interact with each other, it makes sense to make these environments tailored and its members more relevant to each other.

▶ When small businesses are presented in aggregate, it makes sense for a multinational corporation to work with a small business, knowing that the small business has the support structure of a coworking environment behind it.

▶ Menial work will be automated, due to the advent of artificial intelligence, or robotics. Robots allow companies to automate functions which are fundamentally repetitive, so that the team will be freed up to have discussions, provide services and conduct the personal tasks that cannot be automated.

▶ With the growth of coworking comes the need for better organisational support from broad associations that can better advocate for workers and owners with local, state and federal governments.

WAYS TO ENGAGE WITH COWORKING ENVIRONMENTS

The coworking industry emerged from a deep dissatisfaction with the physical environment of real estate and has evolved over the last decade into a far more comprehensive, far more inclusive and far more successful real estate solution than leasing alone. But coworking continues to move forward in accordance with innovative new ideas, technological advances and changes in the global and local economies. Real estate finally aligns with the pace of business today and the legacy of the coworking industry will be a world that more closely resembles the environment that we need to thrive and succeed in, while leaving a much finer ecological footprint.

At the beginning of this book, I opened rather glibly with a chapter entitled, 'What You Think You Know about Coworking Is Most Likely Wrong.' If you got this far, I really hope that doesn't apply anymore. Moreover, I hope you can now see that not only is coworking here to stay, it's the defining trend in real estate for this generation.

Perhaps you're excited about coworking and you want to see how you or your organisation could leverage coworking or how your building could benefit from having a coworking space, but you're currently questioning, 'What do I do? What are the next steps?' Here is my answer to that question: The first thing you don't do is go and build your own coworking space.

If you've learned anything from this book, please take away that coworking is a multi-faceted and complex industry that is incredibly high touch and vastly more sophisticated than simply fitting out an office beautifully. As I've learned, to run a coworking space effectively requires an entirely different temperament of management than the traditional asset management approach to buildings. But, there are plenty of ways to get involved.

In this final chapter, we're going to look at flexi-work programmes, opportunities for engagement partnerships, outernships (which is a backwards way of doing an internship) and finally, how to start to explore the new real estate framework for businesses. We will discuss how to use coworking as part of a well thought out real estate solution to maximise efficiency, maximise employee experience and minimise cost. The latter section forms the preface of my next book, so you get a teaser.

FLEXI-WORK PROGRAMMES

Being able to work flexibly - to choose your own work time and location - consistently ranks as the most important consideration when Gen Y employees choose a job. Large organisations are not immune to this trend; the challenge is that it has been more expensive for a large business to administer flexi-work programmes than it has been to maintain their traditional nine-to-five working style.

With the advent of coworking, it's now suddenly possible for large portions of a workforce to work closer to home, or in an environment that employees find more conducive to working - perhaps one that is more social or engaging. These qualities improve workplace happiness and can be achieved through flexi-work programmes.

Recently, two major organisations have taken up flexi-work options in Hong Kong and in New York. HSBC Bank in Hong Kong decided to purchase 300 coworking subscriptions with a major coworking operator in Hong Kong, allowing their employees to work flexibly across two very central locations. These creative and flexible environments in effect expose their employees to their clients and to the small businesses they're serving.

In New York, Microsoft did the same with about 300 memberships spread across seven locations. All of the coworking environments have a general proximity around Microsoft's corporate headquarters in New York. This strategy provides a mixture and a diversity of working environments to suit the complexity of the company's workforce.

A coworking or flexi-work model, as opposed to a fixed overhead of someone's work station, can present a massive cost saving to a MNC. Due to the ad hoc nature of coworking and flexible memberships, the shift doesn't have to be a huge commitment. It provides a very easy, low friction, entry point for multinational corporations, giving them a chance to see if coworking is something that they'd like to utilize. They can easily curtail such a trial if it doesn't work out.

ENGAGEMENT PARTNERSHIPS

I use the word 'engagement' because I strongly dislike the word 'sponsorship.' Engagement partnerships are named as such because there could be ways that a multinational corporation, or an organisation that manages a large number of people, can engage in a co-work. If they'd like to engage with an entrepreneurial or startup community, they could do so in a way that is far more effective than simply sponsoring something.

To give you an example, an engagement partnership could be such that the large corporation creates a training program, a series of workshops or talks, so that a small business may access particular knowledge or expertise. In Singapore, I've worked with Price Waterhouse Coopers (PwC) to create engagement programmes for my clients. This step was an unprecedented move to grant access to exceptional financial expertise to early, small-stage businesses. Doing so improves the small business's likelihood of success, helping the business to avoid later-stage pitfalls.

218

Engagement, as opposed to sponsorship, is an opportunity for a large organisation to learn a lot more about the changing landscape of small business. MNCs will understand the way that coworking environments, or aggregate centres of business, run and function. This knowledge is important, because these centres are going to become nodes and very important contact points in the future of their business.

OUTERNSHIPS

Outernships are the new internships. Everybody's familiar with the idea of an internship; when people are in the early stages of their careers, they seek internships with larger organisations to gain credibility and experience. This allows the intern to put the company's name on their CV, thereby increasing their employability. 'Outernships' is a term that I coined, but it's essentially the idea of turning an internship on its head.

What we're seeing now are multinational companies sending their employees out into the startup community to try and capture a little bit of the essence of what's happening in small business. The intention is to bring that dynamism and creative way of working back into a multinational corporation.

At Collective Works, we hosted an innovation team of about twenty outerns in Singapore for a period of three months. These outerns conducted their normal day-to-day business, while learning what it's like to work in a creative and dynamic coworking environment. Then, they tried to take some of the best elements back into their multinational parent company when they returned.

There are many things that PLRD businesses do very well and in some ways better than large organisations. Their advantage is how affordable it is for them to experiment and play, compared to the cost of research and development in large organisations. They are able to innovate and change technology and to develop new systems and ways of working, because they are less regulated than multinational companies. The benefit of an outernship is multifold; I think the only risk is that the outerns may enjoy their experience a little bit too much.

DECENTRALISED OFFICE SPACES

The deepest way for a company to engage with a coworking environment is to consider decentralizing the real estate of their business. There are organisations, even large multinational corporations, asking if they should maintain the fixed real estate base that they have now, or if they should consider consolidating their team back to an immovable core - which is typically finance and maybe IT - and decentralizing the rest of the team.

Typically, when a large corporation adds up the cost of their corporate real estate - depreciation, operating overheads and their real estate team - and divides that by the number of employees they have, the cost for providing workspace per head can be in the region of $2,500 to $5,000 per month. This is an astonishing fixed overhead cost that most of the world's multinational companies carry. Compare that rate to a coworking environment, which can provide fully-serviced accommodation to its team members for somewhere between $700 and $1,000 per head. That's almost a 50 percent savings against what companies are able to do for their teams in their own space.

Why is that difference so big? The answer is legacy culture and behaviours leading to a fit-for-all approach. No one in a multinational corporation is incentivised in quite the same way as a coworking operator so they deliver different outcomes. When large companies build their own offices, they approach the space from a luxury and branding perspective; they're very generous with their space provisions. They end up paying for meeting room space and void space that are non-functioning or non-revenue generating.

If more large organisations actually sat down and looked at their fixed real estate costs and what they could be able to do if they worked with a global coworking operator, or a network of coworking operators like LExC, they would consider reducing real estate. Instead, most large companies entertain the traditional cost-cutting mechanisms of reducing headcount and losing knowledge. At this stage, only the most courageous companies are considering this shift to coworking and Cisco is the organisation worldwide that's really leading the charge.

In many cities worldwide, Cisco has put their teams into coworking environments rather than their headquarters. What they've realised is that, as a tech-enabled company, they need to practise what they preach. They need to live a mobile, connected lifestyle using global mobility phones, remote connection computers, video conferencing and other advanced telephony that help people connect in natural ways over vast distances.

Members of LExC get five days free in every LExC space, worldwide - there are forty LExC spaces in U.S. cities at the moment and an additional thirty spaces in international cities worldwide - everywhere from Buenos Aires, Paris, London and San Francisco to Singapore and several cities in Australia.

Cisco is therefore a business that has bet the family silver on a global way of working. They've done so because they're aware of the emerging trends, but also because, by being end users of their own hardware and software, they're able to experience first-hand how effective or ineffective it is and to create informed decisions. The company is living and proving the effectiveness and efficiency of their own software.

CHAPTER ELEVEN TAKEAWAYS

▶ Effectively running a coworking space requires an entirely different temperament of management than the traditional asset management approach to buildings. But, there are plenty of ways to get involved in the coworking model.

▶ A coworking or flexi-work model can present a massive cost saving to a MNC. It provides a very easy, low friction, entry point for multinational corporations, giving them a chance to see if coworking is something that they'd like to utilize.

▶ Engagement, as opposed to sponsorship, is an opportunity for a large organisation to learn a lot more about the changing landscape of small business. MNCs will understand the way that coworking environments, or aggregate centres of business, run and function.

▶ Multinational companies can send their employees into the startup community through 'outernships' at coworking environments. The intention is to bring dynamism and a creative way of working back into the multinational corporation.

▶ The deepest way for a company to engage with a coworking environment is to consider decentralizing the real estate of their business. This can lead to significant cost saving.

ABOUT THE AUTHOR

Jonathan O'Byrne is the founder of Collective Works, one of Singapore's founding coworking networks. His work focuses on building thriving coworking environments for his high performing business clients. Having launched Singapore's first CBD coworking environment, Jonathan's business has expanded rapidly and in 2016 entered into a landmark joint venture agreement with CapitaLand to develop coworking spaces.

Jonathan has become known throughout the industry as a thought leader in coworking, recently keynoting at Coworking Unconference Asia 2017 and 2016 and speaking at Global Coworking Unconference Conference China (GCUC China) in Dec 2015 and hosting the GCUC Singapore conference in Nov 2017. He has succeeded in creating an unparalleled entrepreneurial community of over

200 companies (to date) from entrepreneurs to SMEs and MNCs with members from over forty-seven countries. In October 2014, Collective Works was awarded the Small Business Rising Star Award at the 15th Annual Business Awards, praising Collective Works as a 'true market leader in its sector.'

A lifelong expatriate, born in Europe before moving overseas, Jonathan has lived on three continents, moving to Singapore in 2010. The concept for Collective Works was borne out of his experiences in his own working life. Jonathan saw a problem: the isolation inherent in entrepreneurship and the need to promote collaboration amongst like-minded people. He realised that by facilitating connections he could not only create a paradigm shift in the quality of people's working lives but what they were able to achieve as well. The solution became the catalyst and inspiration for Collective Works.

Known for his keen eye for innovative design, Jonathan attended London's prestigious Central Saint Martins College of Art & Design, before undertaking a BA (Hons) at London College of Fashion. Jonathan's work is rooted in the belief that design can improve the way people experience the world through a focus on human experience. Through Collective Works Jonathan is providing a support system for businesses and a building collaborative eco-system of like-minded entrepreneurs.

SOURCES

1 https://www.universitiesuk.ac.uk/facts-and-stats/data-and-analysis/Pages/patterns-and-trends-uk-higher-education-2013.aspx

2 https://www.bls.gov/spotlight/2012/recession/pdf/recession_bls_spotlight.pdf

3 http://www.deskmag.com/en/the-history-of-coworking-spaces-in-a-timeline

4 https://impacthub.net/locations/

5 https://www.dropbox.com/s/rjbmdo4wp4aeccx/2018%20Complete%20Coworking%20Forecast.pdf?dl=0

6 http://gcuc.co/wp-content/uploads/2017/12/GCUC-Global-Coworking-Stats-2017-2022.pdf

7 https://www.indexmundi.com/spain/demographics_profile.html

8 https://www.focus-economics.com/blog/spains-youth-in-labor-marketdian

9 http://www.nycedc.com/sites/default/files/filemanager/Resources/Studies/Commercial_Real_Estate_Competitiveness_Study.pdf

10 https://www.fidi.org/blog/real-cost-expatriate-assignment-failure

11 https://www.fidi.org/blog/5-biggest-reasons-expatriate-failure

Printed in Poland
by Amazon Fulfillment
Poland Sp. z o.o., Wrocław